1-80

❦ THE ❦
KINGS AND QUEENS
OF SCOTLAND

THE KINGS & QUEENS OF SCOTLAND

Caroline Bingham

WEIDENFELD AND NICOLSON
LONDON

Weidenfeld and Nicolson
11 St John's Hill, London SW11

ISBN 0 297 77043 8
Printed and bound in Great Britain by
Morrison & Gibb Ltd, London and Edinburgh

❦ Contents

To Elisabeth Russell Taylor

⚱ Illustrations

King James IV, drawing by Jacques le Boucq, from the *Recueil d'Arras* (*Bibliothèque Municipale, Arras*)

King James V and Madeleine of France, from the *Seton Armorial* (*National Library of Scotland; loaned by Sir David Ogilvy Bt*)

Miniature of King James V, by an unknown artist (*Scottish National Portrait Gallery*)

Marie de Guise, detail from a contemporary double portrait of her with King James V (*National Trust; picture at Hardwick Hall, Derbyshire*)

Mary, Queen of Scots, portrait by an unknown artist (*National Portrait Gallery*)

King James VI as a child, attributed to Rowland Lockey (*National Portrait Gallery*)

King James VI and I in Garter robes, by Daniel Mytens (*National Portrait Gallery*)

Miniature of James VI and I on the Lyte Jewel, attributed to Nicholas Hilliard (*British Museum, Waddesdon bequest*)

Anne of Denmark, portrait attributed to William Larkin (*National Portrait Gallery*)

King Charles I, triple portrait by Van Dyck (*by gracious permission of HM the Queen; picture in the Royal Collection at Windsor*)

Henrietta Maria, portrait from the studio of Van Dyck (*Scottish National Portrait Gallery*)

King Charles II, portrait after J.M. Wright (*National Portrait Gallery*)

King James VII and II, portrait by Sir Peter Lely (*Scottish National Portrait Gallery*)

Queen Anne, detail from portrait by Michael Dahl (*National Portrait Gallery*)

Queen Mary II, portrait after William Wissing (*National Portrait Gallery*)

King William 'III' with a candle, portrait by Gottfried Schalcker (*National Trust; picture at Pittingham*)

King James 'VIII and III', portrait by Trevasini (*Blairs College, Aberdeen*)

Maria Clementina Sobieska, miniature by an unknown artist (*Collection of Mr Peter Maxwell Stuart of Traquair; photograph by Richard Tilbrook*)

Prince Charles Edward Stuart, by Louis-Gabriel Blanchet (*by gracious permission of HM the Queen; picture at Holyrood*)

Prince Henry Benedict Stuart, Cardinal-Duke of York, portrait after Batoni (*National Portrait Gallery*)

The maps on pages xiii–xv were designed by Tony Cullimore.

🍀 Author's Note

Readers of this book will notice that Part Four is entitled 'The House of Stewart 1371–1603', and Part Five 'The House of Stuart 1603–1707'. The surname of the royal House which ruled Scotland as a separate kingdom was spelled 'Stewart', the name deriving from the office of High Steward of Scotland held by the family in its pre-royal centuries. The spelling 'Stuart' is merely the French variant used by Mary, Queen of Scots, who was brought up in France, and by other members of the family who had French connections: the Franco-Scottish Stuarts of Aubigny and the descendants of Matthew Stuart, fourth Earl of Lennox, who took French nationality in 1537. Lord Darnley, Lennox's son, who married Mary, Queen of Scots, was thus a 'Stuart', and their son James VI and I was therefore a 'Stuart' not a 'Stewart'. However, he is usually referred to as a member of the 'Stewart' dynasty of Scotland and as the first of the 'Stuart' kings of England – inconsistent but convenient.

THE MAKING OF SCOTLAND

The coalescence of Scots, Picts, Britons and Angles produced the Scottish people, with the Norse-dominated isles as later additions to the Kingdom.

Shetland

NORSE

NORSE

Orkney

NORSE

NORSE

P I C T L A N D

Moray Firth

PICTS

Iona

SCOTS

DALRIADA

Firth of Forth

LOTHIAN

Lindis-farne.

ANGLES

STRATHCLYDE

Firth of Clyde

BRITONS

Border undelineated

NORTHUMBRIA

Solway Firth

TOPOGRAPHICAL MAP
OF SCOTLAND

SHETLAND

ORKNEY

Pentland Firth

Cape Wrath

Moray Firth

Kinloss

Peterhead

NORTH
UIST

Inverness

SKYE

SOUTH
UIST

Aberdeen

ERISKAY

Glenshiel

Braemar

Glenfinnan

Loch
Shiel

Fort William

Brechin

Montrose

Glencoe

Dunkeld

Arbroath

ISLE OF
IONA

Oban

Ruthven Castle
(Huntingtower)

Scone

St Andrews

Perth

KERRERA

Inveraray

Dunblane

Loch
Leven

Falkland

ISLE OF
MAY

Dunbarton

Stirling

Dunfermline

Cambuskenneth

Firth of Forth

Dunbar

Linlithgow

Renfrew

Edinburgh

Holyrood

BUTE

Rothesay

Glasgow

Newbattle

Berwick

Lauder

KINTYRE

Melrose

Kelso

Birgham

Dryburgh

Roxburgh

Ayr

Jedburgh

Lochmaben

Dumfries

Dundrennan

Solway Firth

Whithorn

BATTLES IN THE
HISTORY OF SCOTLAND

CAITHNESS

Carbisdale
1649 ✗

ROSS

MORAY   BUCHAN

✗ Culloden
    1746

MAR

ATHOLL
                    ANGUS
        ✗ Killiecrankie
            1689   Nechtansmere
                        685 ✗

GOWRIE   ✗ Dunkeld
                1045

STRATHEARN ✗ Dupplin Moor
                1332

            Sherriffmuir   FIFE
MENTEITH   ✗ 1715
    Sauchieburn ✗ ✗ Bannockburn
        1488   1314
        Falkirk ✗   Prestonpans ✗ Dunbar
        1298 & 1746 LOTH Pinkie ✗ 1745   1296 & 1650
    Langside   1547 ✗ I A N
    1568 ✗   Rullion Green   ✗ Halidon Hill
✗ Largs   Bothwell ✗   1666 ✗ Carberry   1333 ✗
  1263   Bridge 1679 ✗ Stirling Bridge Hill 1567
                        1297   Carham-on-Tweed
        Loudoun ✗ ✗ Drumclog   1018 ✗ ✗ Flodden
        Hill 1307 1679   1513
                            ✗ Philiphaugh Homildon
                                1645   1402

CARRICK GALLOWAY

            ✗ Arkinholme
                1455

            ✗ Solway Moss
                1542
                        Neville's Cross
                        1346 ✗

                'Battle of the Standard' ✗
                (Northallerton) · 1138

1

CALEDONIA
BECOMES SCOTLAND

🦢 Tribes and Kingdoms

The Roman Province of Britannia did not comprise the whole mainland of Britain. It covered roughly the area which centuries later became the kingdom of England. To the north of the Roman Province lay the wild and unconquered land of Caledonia.

The first Roman to attempt the conquest of Caledonia was Gnaeus Julius Agricola, the Governor of Britannia, who ascertained that Britain was an island and aspired to make the northern coastline the frontier of the province.

His offensive provoked a great confederacy of tribes under the leadership of Calgacus – who was clearly a great chief though not a King – and he defeated the tribal army at the battle of Mons Graupius in AD 83. Agricola's success, followed by his immediate recall to Rome, inspired Tacitus's famous words: *'Britannia perdomita et statim amissa'* – 'Britain wholly conquered and at once thrown away'.

The same thing was to happen over and over again in Scottish history. Invaders from the south would win an overwhelming victory, but the advantage of war would still remain with the inhabitants of an impossible terrain. A victory in the Lowlands did not presuppose the conquest of a country full of mountains and mountainous ranges of hills. (It is here worth mentioning that the 'Highland Line' is not an east-west division, but one extending from the north-east to the south-west, so that most of the eastern seaboard can be regarded as lowland.)

After Agricola's withdrawal, the Romans preferred a policy of containment and limited infiltration to one of conquest. Hadrian built his great wall from the Tyne to the Solway in AD 121, and twenty years later the Governor Lollius Urbicus attempted to establish a more northerly frontier and built the Antonine Wall from the Forth to the Clyde. The last offensive came in 208 when the old Emperor Severus marched as far as the shore of the Moray Firth, spreading destruction and terror, and then retired south again to die at York.

In the end the Romans contented themselves by trying merely to contain the northern tribes. Hadrian's Wall marked the frontier, though some military outposts were maintained further north. Caledonia had experienced the aggression but not the civilization of Rome.

The later Romans knew the names of some seventeen northern tribes, but they were inclined to refer to the dwellers beyond the wall in general terms as 'Caledonii' or 'Picti'.

In 407 the Roman army was withdrawn from Britannia, for the north-westernmost province of the Empire had to be abandoned when Rome itself was threatened by internal chaos and barbarian invasion. Romano-British civilization went down before the attacks of seaborne Teutonic invaders.

From the convulsions of what are still traditionally called the Dark Ages emerged the new civilization of Anglo-Saxon England, with its several kingdoms which play only an incidental part in the present narrative.

The north of the island was divided between four peoples whose kingdoms ultimately contributed to the making of Scotland. Predominant in this quadripartite arrangement were the Picts, whose name the Romans had used so indiscriminately. They were of Celtic stock, but mysterious in their origins as in their later disappearance. Pictland, the largest of the four kingdoms, extended lengthwise from Orkney to the Forth.

To the south of the Picts, the area which is now Lothian was occupied by Anglian invaders who pushed northwards from Northumbria. When the power of Northumbria was at its height, its king, Egfrith, aspired to dominate his northern neighbours. He invaded Pictland and was defeated at the battle of Nechtansmere, near Dunnichen in Forfarshire, by Brude, King of the Picts, in 685. Some historians consider that this battle was decisive in saving the proto-Scotland from Anglian conquest.

The south-western area of the country, between the Clyde and the Solway, with an area south of the Solway extending into

Cumbria, comprised the kingdom of Strathclyde, which was inhabited by Welsh-speaking Britons.

The area which is now Argyll, with its adjacent islands, was known as Dalriada, and the Scots who inhabited it were the people destined ultimately to dominate the rest. It is one of the apparent absurdities of history, and therefore easily remembered, that Ireland was called 'Scotia' before it was called Ireland, and that the Scots came from Ireland and colonized Scotland. The Scots, who were Gaelic-speaking Celts, had probably been colonizing Argyll for over a century before they acquired a king, in the person of Fergus Mor mac Erc.

This first King of the Scots, who came of royal blood in Ireland, left the parent kingdom of Irish Dalriada (roughly coterminous with County Antrim) to found a new kingdom in about the year 500. From him all the subsequent kings of Scotland could claim descent. In the Middle Ages a legendary pedigree was invented for him, which traced his forbears back to one Fergus, son of Ferehard, who was supposed to have flourished in about 330 BC. However, descent from Fergus Mor mac Erc himself conferred a sufficiently prestigious antiquity upon the successive Scottish dynasties, for though their descent from Fergus grew tenuous, it remained unbroken. When one royal House failed in the male line, it was through a female that the succeeding House claimed the kingship. The blood of Fergus flowed through the early royal Houses of Alpin and Dunkeld, to those of Bruce and Stewart, and at last, through the person of James vi and i's daughter Elizabeth, it was transmitted to the House of Hanover.

Just over sixty years after the arrival of Fergus, a great man of a very different kind came to Dalriada from Ireland. In 563 St Columba, who was also of royal descent, established his famous monastery on the island of Iona. He found the Scots of Dalriada already Christian. Fergus and his kindred had probably come from Ireland as converts of St Patrick. Some centuries later it was indeed claimed that St Patrick had prophesied the kingship of Fergus and the royal destiny of his descendants.

St Columba was not only an outstanding religious leader, he

was also an astute politician. He lent his influence both morally and politically to the royal House of Dalriada and greatly strengthened the kingdom in its relations with its more powerful neighbour Pictland. His great work as a missionary was to advance the conversion of the Picts.

St Columba was not indeed the first Christian missionary, for St Ninian had established his church at Whithorn, beside Wigtown Bay, before the end of the fourth century. By the end of the seventh century, through the labours of many missionary saints, all four northern kingdoms had accepted Christianity, and this community of religion must have helped to make possible the first of the political unions which led to the foundation of Scotland.

In 843 the Scots and the Picts were united under Kenneth mac Alpin, King of Scots; thenceforward the kingdom ruled by Kenneth and his descendants was known as Scotia. Its Gaelic name of Alba or Albainn survived in the name of the later Scottish dukedom of Albany.

❦ *The House of Alpin*

Among the Picts the law of succession was matrilineal, and it was presumably through the marriage of a Pictish princess into the royal House of Dalriada that Kenneth mac Alpin derived his claim to the kingship of the Picts.

He is said to have been a man of 'marvellous astuteness', and since he succeeded in uniting two peoples between whom there had been much enmity, that comment upon his character is probably accurate. However, he may have been not only astute but also ruthless, for apparently in consequence of their union with the Scots, the Picts tacitly disappeared from the pages of history.

It is probable that Kenneth pressed his claim to the kingship of the Picts by force of arms, but the darker rumour was repeated by the late twelfth-century historian Giraldus Cambrensis that Kenneth assured the dominance of his own people by massacring the Pictish nobility. Either way it seems scarcely explicable that

Pictish culture should have been extinguished as completely as it was.

It may be that the destruction of the Picts was the work not of the Scots but of the Vikings, for the union of the kingdoms under Kenneth occurred at a time when the whole of Britain was suffering from the aptly named 'fury of the Northmen'.

The Vikings came to plunder but remained to settle and eventually to become Christian. The newly founded Scotia was soon surrounded by Norse settlements. Orkney, Shetland and the Western Isles remained Norse-dominated for centuries, and other settlements were made on the west coast of the Scottish mainland, and farther south in Cumbria. Then, just over twenty years after Kenneth had united his two kingdoms, York fell to the Vikings, cutting off the country to the north of it from the rest of Anglo-Saxon England and leaving Lothian a debatable land, vulnerable to the Scots if they had the strength to take it.

Kenneth mac Alpin, though he was a strong king within his own territories, was clearly not strong enough to effect the conquest of Lothian. Six invasions did not suffice to bring it under his rule, and it was left to the last of his line to unite it to the kingdom.

Though matrilinealism had brought a Scottish king to the Pictish throne, this custom disappeared together with all other aspects of Pictish culture. The history, legends and customs of the Scots became the common heritage of the kingdom, the Scottish law of succession among the rest.

The Scottish succession was decided by tanistry. According to this system any mature male of the royal kindred was eligible for the kingship if he were *rígdomnae* – 'the stuff of kings'. In the hope, usually a vain hope, that the warring ambitions of royal kinsmen would not lead to recurrent bloodshed, the king's successor was nominated during his lifetime, and he became the tanist, the *tanaise ríg* or 'Second to the King'. Long after succession by primogeniture had become established in Scotland, the heir presumptive would be referred to as the 'Second Person' of the kingdom, a style which surely preserves an echo of the older system.

Succession by tanistry remained the rule among the descendants of Kenneth mac Alpin for the two centuries during which
the House of Alpin endured. It is illustrated by Genealogical
Table No 1, but the following king-list may help to clarify the
order of succession :

KINGS OF THE HOUSE OF ALPIN

Kenneth I mac Alpin, 843–59.

Donald I, 859–63 (brother of Kenneth).

Constantine I, 863–77 (elder son of Kenneth).

Aed, 877–8 (younger son of Kenneth).

Eochaid, 878–89 (nephew of Aed).

Donald II, 889–900 (son of Constantine I).

Constantine II, 900–42 (son of Aed).

Malcolm I, 942–54 (son of Donald II).

Indulf, 954–62 (son of Constantine II).

Dubh, 962–7 (elder son of Malcolm I).

Cuilean, 967–71 (son of Indulf).

Kenneth II, 971–95 (younger son of Malcolm I).

Constantine III, 995–7 (son of Cuilean).

Kenneth III, 997–1005 (son of Dubh).

Malcolm II, 1005–34 (son of Kenneth II).

Despite the way in which the succession was tossed to and fro
among the royal kindred, the last of the fifteen kings of the
House of Alpin was as directly descended from the first as
though the crown had come to him by simple primogeniture.
Malcolm II was Kenneth mac Alpin's great-great-great-great-
grandson.

For the most part these early kings of Scots are shadowy
figures, like the majority of their southern counterparts the
Anglo-Saxon Kings of England. Nonetheless, during these half-
forgotten reigns certain events occurred which were decisive in
shaping Scotland's future.

Kenneth mac Alpin, seeking to strengthen his grip on Pictish
territory, established his seat of government at Scone, which was
to become the traditional coronation place of the Scottish kings.
To Scone he brought the palladium of the Scots, the 'Stone of

Destiny', which from its long residence there also came to be called the 'Stone of Scone'. By tradition the kings of Scots were ceremonially seated upon the sacred stone as part of the ritual of their inauguration. The stone was an object of legend and super-stition. Legend made it the stone which had been Jacob's pillow at Bethel, and which had been brought from the Holy Land to Ireland by the remote ancestors of the Scots, and from Ireland to Scotland by Fergus Mor mac Erc. Superstition credited it with the power to carry the rule of a Scottish king wherever it was placed. There was a Gaelic prophecy to this effect:

> *Cinnidh Sgoit saor am fine*
> *Mur breug am faistine;*
> *Far am faighear an Lia-Fail*
> *Dlighe flaitheas do ghabhail.*

> [Scots shall flourish strong and free
> Unless proved false the prophecy;
> That where the Stone shall yet be found
> A Scot by princely right is crowned.]

A Latin version of these words was said to have been carved on the Stone itself:

> *Ni fallat fatam, Scoti, quocunque locatum,*
> *Invenient lapidem, regnare tenentur ibidem.*

It was likewise Kenneth mac Alpin who sought to remove the spiritual centre of the country from the far west, by bringing the relics of St Columba from Iona to Dunkeld. In 943 Constantine II moved them again, this time to the monastery at St Andrews whither he had abdicated. Though Iona always retained a certain numinosity, St Andrews became the spiritual capital of the king-dom, and centuries later, in the reign of James III, the primatial see.

Edinburgh, the future secular capital, was still outside the kingdom, in the debatable land of Lothian. The great defensible rock, so excellent a site for a fortress, was captured by King Indulf, but Lothian itself was not conquered until 1018 when Malcolm II annexed it after his victory at Carham on the Tweed.

After the brief and bloody reigns of some of his predecessors, Malcolm ɪɪ's reign of almost thirty years shows that at least he possessed a formidable talent for survival, the more so that in an age when life was frequently 'nasty, brutish and short', he was over eighty years old when he died. His record suggests that he may have possessed the same 'marvellous astuteness' as the founder of his line.

Malcolm ɪɪ's grandson Duncan became King of Strathclyde, as one of a line of Scottish sub-Kings of the small neighbouring kingdom. When Malcolm died in 1034, Duncan succeeded him, and thus the kingdoms of Scotia, Lothian and Strathclyde were at last united. Though the Western Isles did not become subject to the kings of Scots until the thirteenth century, nor Orkney and Shetland until the fifteenth, and though the frontier with England remained long undefined, the northern kingdom had recognizably become Scotland.

Appropriately, it is at this moment in history that the proverbial mists of antiquity disperse to reveal some very familiar figures, for Duncan ɪ of Scotland was the king destined to be slain by Macbeth.

2
THE HOUSE OF DUNKELD
1034–1290

❦ Shakespearean Characters

On the death of Malcolm II, the House of Alpin failed in the male line. Malcolm had two daughters, and the only surviving descendant of his cousin and immediate predecessor Kenneth III was a grand-daughter. King Malcolm's grandsons and King Kenneth's grand-daughter were the leading characters in the drama with which the history of the new dynasty opened.

Malcolm's elder daughter Bethoc married Crinan 'the Thane', lay abbot of Dunkeld. At this period, when Celtic monasticism was in decline, lay abbots appear to have been as accepted a part of the ecclesiastical structure as they became centuries later on the eve of the Reformation. Crinan was a great nobleman, as his title implies, and he possessed the added prestige of belonging to the kindred of St Columba. It was from his abbacy of Dunkeld that the new royal House took its name, for Crinan and Bethoc were the parents of King Duncan I.

Malcolm's younger daughter, whose name may have been Donada, married Finlaech, Mormaer of Moray (Mormaer was a Celtic title which appears to have been the equivalent of Thane or Earl), and they were the parents of Macbeth, who was therefore Duncan's first cousin. His name was in fact 'Maelbeatha', though it would be somewhat pedantic to revert to it.

Macbeth married Kenneth III's grand-daughter Gruoch, the original of Shakespeare's Lady Macbeth. Gruoch had been previously married to Gillacomgan, Mormaer of Moray, a cousin of Macbeth's father Finlaech. By her first marriage she had a son named Lulach.

The events in which Duncan, Macbeth and Gruoch took part were different in emphasis and timing from the familiar events of Shakespeare's tragedy.

Duncan was quite young, probably about thirty-three, when he succeeded his grandfather. At the time of his death in 1040 his two sons, Malcolm and Donald *Ban* (or Donalbain), were small children.

Macbeth, who was slightly younger than his cousin the King, had, according to the rule of tanistry, an equally good claim to the throne by right of birth, though Duncan had apparently succeeded as their grandfather's chosen heir. In 1040 Macbeth asserted his claim by force of arms, slew Duncan in battle and made himself king.

There is no knowing whether Gruoch's influence played any part in these events. She and Macbeth had no children, but it is likely that as the years passed, she may have become anxious to see her son Lulach accepted as his stepfather's heir.

Duncan's Queen had been a kinswoman of Siward, the Danish Earl who governed northern England under Edward the Confessor. Upon Duncan's death his elder son Malcolm was sent for safety to Siward's Court at York, and subsequently to the Court of the English king; the younger son Donald *Ban* was sent to the Western Isles, and then possibly to Ireland. The 'separated fortune' of the brothers, to which Shakespeare referred, was to lead to separate interests and ultimately to bitter enmity.

Meanwhile, Macbeth consolidated his triumph by defeating and slaying Duncan's father, Crinan, in a battle at Dunkeld in 1045.

Bloodshed, if not murder, had made him king, but he ruled successfully for seventeen years. He was an outstanding benefactor of the Church, and his rule was strong enough to permit his making a pilgrimage to Rome in 1050, where it was recorded that he 'scattered money among the poor like seed'.

Macbeth appeared to be liberal and secure, but he had an enemy whom the years could only make more dangerous. In 1054 Malcolm, with the assistance of his kinsman Siward, invaded Scotland, defeated Macbeth at Scone and wrested Lothian and Cumbria from him. (The name Cumbria was now given to the whole area which had previously been the kingdom of Strathclyde.) Three years later Malcolm invaded again and completed his victory when he defeated and slew Macbeth at Lumphanan in Aberdeenshire, in 1057.

Malcolm still had Lulach to deal with. Lulach was called 'the Simple', so possibly it is permissible to see the influence of Gruoch behind his coronation at Scone immediately upon the death of his stepfather. But early the following year Malcolm slew him, it was said, 'by strategy'. At the end of Shakespeare's play Malcolm, on his way to his coronation at Scone, refers to Macbeth and his wife with pious horror as 'this dead butcher and his fiend-like Queen', but perhaps when Malcolm became King of Scots, his hands were no less bloodstained than Macbeth's.

Malcolm Ceann Mor *and Saint Margaret*

King Malcolm III was known as *Ceann Mor*, which is customarily translated as 'Bighead'. Only one historian has suggested that 'head' in this context bears the same meaning as in 'headman', so that *Ceann Mor* ought to be translated as 'Great Chief'. This suggestion appears to have the merit of inherent probability.

In character Malcolm was a ferocious warrior yet a man who was capable of responding to civilizing influences. Though he could neither read nor write, he spoke Gaelic, English and Latin.

Malcolm's first wife was Ingeborg of Orkney, who was either the widow or the daughter of the Norse Earl Thorfinn. By her Malcolm had three children, of whom the eldest son later reigned as Duncan II.

Malcolm had been on the throne for eight years when William, Duke of Normandy, invaded England, won the battle of Hastings and had himself crowned King of England on Christmas Day 1066. The first result of the Norman Conquest in Scotland was that it threw upon Malcolm's mercy two exalted refugees: Edgar the Athling (i.e. the Anglo-Saxon heir to the English throne) and his sister Margaret, who was to take her place in history as St Margaret of Scotland.

Malcolm married Margaret as his second wife in 1069. She may well have been beautiful in person and in character, for she captivated Malcolm at once and inspired in him a lifelong devotion. She was certainly devout, civilized and strong-minded. For her charity, humanity and asceticism, and for her services to the

Church, she was canonized in 1251, but she was popularly regarded as a saint in her own lifetime.

Margaret's confessor Turgot wrote a *Life* of the Queen, designed to display her saintly qualities. It contains a touching description of Malcolm's love and reverence for his wife:

> He readily obeyed her wishes and prudent counsels in all things. Whatever she refused, he refused also; whatever pleased her, he also loved for love of her. Hence it was that, although he could not read, he would turn over and examine books which she used either for her devotions or her study; and whenever he heard her express especial liking for a particular book, he would also look at it with special interest, kissing it, and often taking it into his hands. Sometimes he sent for a worker in precious metals, whom he commanded to ornament that volume with gold and gems, and when the work was finished, the King himself used to carry the book to the Queen as a loving proof of his devotion.

Though Margaret was English by birth, her upbringing had been at the Court of Hungary, and the cultural influence which she brought to Scotland was not that of dying Anglo-Saxon England but that of the early flowering of medieval Europe.

To Malcolm's Court, which had hitherto been more like that of a great tribal chief than that of a European king, Margaret brought good manners (always a touchstone of civilization), splendour and a greater use of ceremonial, which could only serve to enhance the prestige of Scotland among the kingdoms of Christendom.

In ecclesiastical matters Margaret's contribution was greatly to increase the direct influence of Rome in Church affairs. It is worth remarking that to refer to the 'Celtic Church' and the 'Roman Church' is to imply that they were completely separate and opposed, which is misleading. At this date the Church of Rome was the universal Church of Western Christendom, from which the Church in Celtic countries differed not in doctrine but in local organization and minor practices.

Margaret set herself to import Roman organization and to

iron out Celtic irregularities. The effect of her reforms, in the Church as in the Court, was to draw Scotland inwards from the Celtic fringe and to make it increasingly participant in the life of western Europe.

Malcolm and Margaret had six sons, four of whom reigned as kings of Scotland. All but one unquestioningly accepted Margaret's ideas, and the last in particular built upon the foundation which she had laid.

Inevitably the europeanizing of Scotland under Margaret and her sons was a slow process. For Malcolm the Norman Conquest of England, though it had brought Margaret to his kingdom, had other and more immediate consequences, both military and political.

Malcolm's ambition was to extend his frontier southwards towards the river Tees. His efforts to do so resembled the efforts of Kenneth mac Alpin to conquer Lothian: in both instances repeated invasion, though destructive, proved unrewarding.

At first it seemed that the Norman Conquest might be to Malcolm's advantage. The wrongs of his brother-in-law Edgar the Athling provided a respectable *casus belli*, and while William of Normandy was consolidating his position in the south of England, the north might fall to Malcolm.

William, however, established his authority more quickly than Malcolm had expected, and in 1072 he marched north with a great army, either to exact submission or to be revenged. Malcolm realized that his resources were not equal to William's. Accordingly, he changed his tactics, received William peaceably at Abernethy and took an oath to be 'his man'. That politic act of homage saved the situation for the present, though it stored up trouble for the future. Not the least of the troubles was caused by Malcolm's sending Duncan, his eldest son by Ingeborg, to the English Court as the pledge of peace.

The peace lasted only until 1079. In that year, and more than once thereafter, Malcolm went to war with England as the aggressor. He lost more than he gained, for his frontier was not advanced, and his ceaseless war-making resulted in William's eldest son Robert 'Curthose' building a 'New Castle' on the river Tyne, and in William's second son and successor William Rufus building another at Carlisle. These defences for the time being marked the eastern and western extremities of the frontier.

In 1093 Malcolm was ambushed and killed at Alnwick, in the course of his fifth invasion of England – this time fully justified by the provocation he had received from Rufus. Margaret, whose penitential practices had undermined her health, was mortally sick in Edinburgh Castle when she received the news of her husband's death, and that of their eldest son Edward, who had been killed with him. Margaret died with saintly composure, expressing her resignation to the will of God.

❦ *Warring Interests*

The death of a strong king let loose the forces of disorder.

The first to take advantage of Malcolm's death was his long-exiled brother, Donald *Ban*. He was aged about sixty, a man whom life had embittered perhaps, but not defeated. *Ban* means 'the fair' or 'the white', so if the epithet were bestowed on him in youth, perhaps he had flaxen-white hair; if in age, he may be imagined as a hoary-headed old King.

Donald *Ban*'s life in the Western Isles, and perhaps in Ireland, had made him, in the words of one historian of the period, 'an incorrigible old Celt'. He had many ready-made adherents, for Margaret's europeanizing policy, which Malcolm had supported, had affected chiefly the Lowlands. Beyond the Highland Line Scotland had its own Celtic fringe, and there Donald *Ban* was popular and approved.

On the death of Malcolm and Margaret, Donald *Ban* attacked Edinburgh Castle. His nephews, who were unprepared, abandoned it, taking their mother's body with them. They buried Margaret at Dunfermline and then fled to England.

At the Court of William Rufus Donald *Ban* was now regarded as the enemy, and the sons of the erstwhile enemy Malcolm were acceptable as refugees. They may have owed this welcome to their half-brother Duncan, who had lived at the English Court since he was handed over as a hostage in 1072 and was in high favour with the King.

William Rufus espoused the cause of Duncan against Donald *Ban*. Rufus had the reputation of an almost archetypal 'bad king' – tyrannous, treacherous, blasphemous and homosexual, 'loathsome to well nigh all his people, and abominable to God' in the words of an English chronicler – but he may have had genuine feelings of friendship for Duncan, whom he had known since childhood. Nonetheless, he did not propose to put him on the throne of Scotland from motives of altruism. He wished to replace an independent Celtic ruler with a pliant vassal king.

Duncan marched north with an Anglo-Norman army, deposed Donald *Ban* and proclaimed himself King Duncan II, in May 1094. He stressed that he was king by right and not conquest, styling himself 'Dunecan, son of King Malcolumb, by hereditary right King of Scotia', in a charter to which one of the signatories was his half-brother Edgar. This shows that he was opposing Donald *Ban*'s claim by tanistry with a claim by primogeniture, and that he had the support of Malcolm's sons by Margaret.

He lacked, however, the support of one of them, Edmund, who was regarded as Margaret's only unworthy son. Edmund made common cause with his uncle Donald *Ban* against Duncan. In November 1094, after a reign of six months, Duncan II was overthrown and murdered. Donald *Ban* and Edmund became joint sovereigns, Donald *Ban* ruling north of the Forth-Clyde line and Edmund south of it.

Their reign lasted three years, but their position was insecure throughout, for they were merely awaiting retaliation by Edmund's brothers, who had the resources of England to draw upon. The brothers were Ethelred, Edgar, Alexander and David. Ethelred had entered the Church, so his claim devolved upon Edgar. Duncan II had a son, whose claim was ignored, for the idea of a minor claiming by primogeniture was insufficiently established to command respect unless it were backed by force. Edgar's claim against Donald *Ban* and Edmund therefore looked much the same as Malcolm III's claim against Macbeth.

But from Edgar onwards the succession was decided by primogeniture.

Edgar purchased English assistance by acknowledging William Rufus as his feudal superior. An army was provided for him, Donald *Ban* and Edmund were deposed and Edgar became king in the autumn of 1097. Edmund was mercifully treated; he was permitted to become a monk. Donald *Ban* was less fortunate. He was captured in 1099, blinded and imprisoned for the remainder of his life. It seems that one act of savagery begat another, for Donald *Ban* is said to have avenged his wrongs by strangling the eldest son of his nephew David. When his life, which had seen such extremes of fortune and misfortune, of suffering and guilt, eventually ended, he was buried at Dunkeld. Subsequently he was reinterred in Iona, among many of the early Celtic kings.

At last, from a period which had witnessed much evil, good began to emerge.

Edgar reigned for nine years and earned himself the epithet of 'the Peaceable'. It may not have been bestowed entirely as a compliment for in 1098 he ceded the Western Isles to Magnus Barelegs, King of Norway, in a passive recognition of a *fait accompli*, which his contemporaries may have considered too peaceable to be consonant with honour. He died unmarried at the beginning of 1107 and was succeeded by his brother, Alexander I.

Edgar had come to the throne as the vassal of William Rufus, but good relations between Scotland and England had ensured that the feudal bond was not humiliating to Scotland. Under Alexander I the vassalage of the Scottish kings appears to have lapsed. Henry I of England married Alexander's sister, whom the English called 'good Queen Maud', and Alexander married Henry's illegitimate daughter Sibylla. The relations of the two Kings, who were at once brothers-in-law and father- and son-in-law, were perhaps too amicable to require legal definition.

Alexander I was a strong king and a devout son of the Church. He won the name of Alexander 'the Fierce' for the fierceness with which he quelled a rebellion in Moray; but he deserved it equally for the fierceness of his determination to defend the independence of the Church in Scotland. Though Scotland lacked an archbishop, Alexander was resolved that the Scottish bishops should not acknowledge the authority of the English Archbishop of York. The question was not solved in Alexander's lifetime. It remained a cause of contention until 1192, when Pope Celestine III declared the Scottish Church to be under the direct protection and jurisdiction of Rome.

Alexander I seems to have been a man who had a taste for splendour and the means to indulge it. The rhyming chronicle of Andrew of Wyntoun gives an account of an exotic offering which he made in the Cathedral of St Andrews:

> *Before the Lordis al the King*
> *Gart thaim* to the altar bring*
> *His cumlie steid of Araby*
> *Saddlit and bridlit costlilie,*
> *Coverit with a fair mantlet*
> *Of precius and of fyn velvett*
> *With his armuris of Turkie . . .*
> *With scheld and speir of silver quyte*
> *And many a precius fair jouell.*

(Wyntoun lived in the late fourteenth and early fifteenth centuries, but he derived his account of this incident from the records of St Andrews.)

Alexander I died without legitimate issue in 1124, to be succeeded by his brother David, the youngest son of Malcolm *Ceann Mor* and St Margaret. The last of a family of remarkably diverse personalities proved to be the greatest.

🦋 David I

The illuminated initial letter of the Charter of Kelso Abbey contains a representation of King David I. The Charter, which was granted in 1159, six years after his death, shows David in old age, a venerable, grey-bearded king, sitting bolt upright on his

* caused them

backless throne, grasping his Sword of State in the manner of a sceptre.

When David I became king, he already had the advantage of experience, for he was forty-four years old at his accession and during the reign of Alexander he had ruled Cumbria and the part of Lothian which lies south of the Lammermuirs.

Besides being the independent ruler of southern Scotland, 'Earl David', as he was then called, was one of the greatest vassals of the English King. His wife, Matilda of Huntingdon, was the grand-daughter of Earl Siward, and through her he obtained the vast territories of the honour of Huntingdon and a claim to her grandfather's earldom of Northumbria.

When he became King of Scots, David, like his father Malcolm *Ceann Mor*, aspired to extend his frontier southwards at England's expense. After the death of Henry I in 1135, the long struggle for the English throne between Henry I's daughter the Empress Maud and her cousin Stephen, Count of Blois, gave David his opportunity.

Maud was David's niece, and at the instance of Henry I, David had taken an oath to support her right to the throne; but Stephen's wife Matilda was also David's niece, the daughter of David's sister Mary, by her husband Eustace, Count of Boulogne (see Genealogical Table No 2). David thus had obligations to both sides, which he discharged by supporting first one and then the other, in accordance with the dictates of his own advantage.

On Henry I's death David seized Carlisle and Newcastle, and three years later, in 1138, he pushed farther south and was defeated near Northallerton in Yorkshire, by an army raised by Thurstan, Archbishop of York. This engagement was called 'the Battle of the Standard', because the English imputed their victory to their religious standard, which was composed of a ship's mast to which was attached a Consecrated Host in a silver pyx and the banners of St Peter of York, St John of Beverley and St Wilfrid of Ripon.

Though David was defeated in battle, Stephen, with whom he made peace, was too hard pressed to exact advantage from the victory. In the treaty signed at Durham in 1139 he yielded to David's son Earl Henry the whole of Northumbria except the fortresses of Newcastle and Bamburgh.

By the end of his reign David I had acquired most of the territory to which Malcolm *Ceann Mor* had aspired in vain: the area which now comprises the English counties of Northumberland, Cumberland and Westmorland had temporarily become part of Scotland.

Within the ancient bounds of his kingdom David's work was more constructive and more enduring. It was the completion in political terms of the europeanizing policy of St Margaret.

David I had spent his formative years at the English Court, and in the England of Henry I he had found much to admire. The Court, which was the administrative centre of the kingdom, had its great officers – the chancellor, chamberlain, constable, steward and marshal – some of whom had been introduced into Scotland by Alexander I. The system of government was feudal, which meant that in theory the king was the actual owner of the whole kingdom, and the great lords who were his tenants-in-chief held their lands in return for giving the king political advice and military service. The lords in turn had their own tenants, who likewise held land in return for military service, while the lower orders in the social hierarchy, tenant farmers and unfree agricultural labourers, in return for their services received security and protection.

David I gained his impressions of the feudal system from England, but it was not an exclusively Anglo-Norman development. It was common to the whole of Christendom, though with innumerable local variations.

To work well, the feudal system demanded a strong awareness of obligations as well as of rights; and since the king was the lynchpin of the whole, it demanded a strong king. David I was such a king, and he recognized that Scotland would benefit from the importation of a system which offered an ideal of order in the place of one in which the savage principle that 'might is right' had previously pertained.

David created a new class of tenants-in-chief by bringing to

Scotland men who already held land from him in England, or
whose friendship he had gained during his years of residence
there. In this way certain great families destined to play leading
parts in Scotland's history – Balliol, Bruce and Stewart among
them – gained their first footholds in the kingdom. David im-
ported his new tenants-in-chief with minimum disruption to the
existing landowners, who became sub-tenants and remained in
possession in return for military service. Most of the newcomers
received fiefs in the Lowlands. In the north-west David endeavoured to implant feudalism by converting the existing Celtic
aristocracy of *mormaers* and *toiseachs* into earls and barons, and
their tribesmen into feudal tenants.

In the course of David's reign a loosely organized Celtic
society became a relatively efficient feudal kingdom. This meta-
morphosis was probably the alternative to conquest or coloniza-
tion by the kings of England. The inability of a Celtic society to
withstand the Anglo-Norman military organization was illustrated by the unhappy histories of Wales and Ireland; but
Scotland's triumphant emergence from the Wars of Independence in the fourteenth century proved the value of David I's
relatively painless Norman Conquest from within.

David I also founded the first Royal Burghs, towns which in
return for an annual payment to the King received the privilege
of conducting foreign trade. He endeavoured to establish uni-
formity of law throughout the kingdom, he instituted the first
uniform system of weights and measures and he issued the first
Scottish coinage.

In ecclesiastical affairs David I showed himself a true son of
St Margaret. Indeed, in his orthodoxy, zeal and admiration for
European forms, if anything he surpassed his mother's example.
He established four communities of Cistercian monks, at
Melrose, Dundrennan, Newbattle and Kinloss, five communities
of Augustinian canons, at Holyrood, Jedburgh, Cambuskenneth,
St Andrews, and on St Serf's Island in Lochleven, and he estab-
lished Tironensians at Kelso, Premonstratensians at Dryburgh
and Cluniacs on the Isle of May.

Monastic communities in the twelfth century provided the

only schools, dispensed charity and practised the most efficient forms of agriculture. Therefore, besides their chief purpose as centres of spiritual life, monastic houses were of great practical value as centres of social service and civilizing influence.

King James I, ruling three hundred years later and struggling with the crippling problem of an empty exchequer, bitterly referred to David I as 'ane sair sanct for the Croun', because he had depleted the Crown's resources by his generosity to the Church. But perhaps James I was looking too far back for the origins of his difficulties. The kings who ruled Scotland in the fortunate thirteenth century were prosperous enough, and David I left his kingdom in a prosperous condition.

The tragedy of his reign occurred in 1152 when his only son, Earl Henry, an able young man who showed the promise of making a good king, predeceased him. David I himself died the following year. The Cistercian chronicler Ailred of Rievaulx, who had been King David's steward before he discovered his vocation to the religious life, wrote an impressive elegy for his late master:

> O desolate Scotia, who shall console thee now? He is no more who made an untilled and barren land a land that is pleasant and plenteous, who adorned thee with castles and cities and lofty towers, enriched thy ports with foreign wares, gathered the wealth of other kingdoms for thine enjoyment, changed thy shaggy cloaks for precious raiment, clothed thine ancient nudity with purple and fine linen, ordered thy barbarous ways with Christian religion.

Ailred's words may have praised the King extravagantly, but he had been a great king, and Scotia may indeed have appeared desolate and vulnerable; for his successor, whom he himself had nominated, was his grandson, the eldest son of Earl Henry, who at the age of eleven succeeded as King Malcolm IV.

The Maiden and the Lion

Malcolm IV is represented beside his grandfather in the initial letter of the Charter of Kelso Abbey. He is portrayed as a fair-haired, beardless youth; he holds a sceptre in his right hand, while the Sword of State lies sheathed across his knees.

Malcolm IV may not have owed his cognomen of 'the Maiden' to an effeminate appearance, as is usually supposed, but to a vow of chastity, for he never married. His contemporaries regarded him as an exceptionally holy youth – 'a terrestrial angel' according to one of them. St Godric, who was an Englishman, declared that the two men living who were most pleasing to God were Malcolm of Scotland and Thomas Becket; if this was a somewhat presumptuous reading of God's mind, at least it put Malcolm on a high level of sanctity.

The year after Malcolm's accession King Stephen of England died. His successor was Henry II, sometimes called Henry FitzEmpress, the son of Maud and the grandson of Henry I. He was an immensely able, violent-tempered man, whose attitude to Scotland was almost as nakedly ambitious as that of his descendant Edward I.

In 1157 Henry II met King Malcolm at Chester and compelled him to restore to England the territories won by David I, merely in return for confirmation of his right to the honour of Huntingdon. Henry could not be blamed for wishing to recover what Stephen had lost, but he conveniently forgot that in 1149, when he himself had wanted help from David I, he had promised that if he became King of England, he would make no attempt to regain Northumbria and in addition would cede Newcastle to the Scots.

Though Malcolm IV lost the coveted land which had been in turn the north of England and the south of Scotland, in Scotland proper he was more successful in defending his rights and the authority of the Crown. Despite the disadvantages of his youth and essentially unwarlike nature, he successfully quelled Celtic rebellions in Galloway, Argyll and Moray; possibly he owed his success to the fact that he had inherited an efficient administration from his grandfather, and in his Norman tenants-in-chief had a reservoir of loyalty to draw upon.

Malcolm IV died at the age of twenty-three in 1165 and was succeeded by his younger brother William, who was a very different personality. Whereas Malcolm had been 'the Maiden', William was 'the Lion'. King William may have acquired this style for a variety of reasons. The most familiar is that he is said to have adopted the lion rampant as the royal arms of Scotland. But also, like Henry I of England, William was known as 'the Lion of Justice' and he was lion-like in his physical strength, for his Gaelic-speaking subjects called him William *Garbh*, or 'the brawny'.

The twenty-two-year-old William bitterly resented that his brother had been forced to cede their grandfather's conquests to Henry II. An opportunity to recover them came when Henry's fortunes were at a low ebb after the murder of Thomas Becket. In 1174, when Henry's sons were in revolt against him, William seized his chance and invaded England. He besieged Carlisle and captured some strongholds in Cumberland and Westmorland but was himself surprised and taken prisoner at Alnwick.

Henry II received the news of King William's capture immediately after he had done penance for the murder of Becket, and he took it as a sign of Divine forgiveness for his sin. He also took full advantage of William's discomfiture. William was imprisoned in the castle of Falaise in Normandy, and there in December 1174 he was forced to acknowledge Henry II as overlord of Scotland. He received his personal freedom in return for the independence of his kingdom, and was permitted to return to Scotland the following year.

Despite his humiliation William ruled well and Scotland prospered. The burghs flourished and the Church was able to maintain its independence against the ambitions of the archbishops of York.

In 1178 William founded the Abbey of Arbroath, which was dedicated to St Thomas Becket. William had been a friend and admirer of Becket, who had been canonized in 1174; no doubt the dedication of Arbroath served both to honour the new saint and to embarrass the King of England.

As the years passed, William, who had several illegitimate children, realized the need to provide Scotland with an heir. In 1186 he married Ermengarde de Beaumont, but a son was not born to them until 1198, when William was fifty-six years old.

In the meantime William had regained his kingdom's independence. In 1189, when Henry II's son and successor Richard *Cœur de Lion* was raising money for the third crusade, William offered him ten thousand merks for the restoration of his sovereign rights. Richard agreed and even admitted that his father had extorted the surrender of them. Scotland once again became a fully sovereign state.

This agreement between the two lion kings, the 'Quitclaim of Canterbury', was completely unambiguous, and claims to overlordship of Scotland made by later English kings had no validity. Nonetheless, the memory that Scottish kings had been the vassals of William the Conqueror and William Rufus was to be a cause of much trouble in the future.

Troubles from the past were revived several times in the reign of William the Lion. In 1179 and 1187, and again in 1211 and 1212, grandsons of Duncan II rebelled in attempts to revive their claim to the throne. The elder was killed in 1187 and the younger betrayed and executed in 1212.

In 1214 King William himself died. His long reign of almost forty-nine years had witnessed extremes of humiliation and triumphant recovery; at the last fortune favoured him, for he lived long enough to see his late-born son Alexander grow into a mature and promising prince.

🐉 *Alexander II*

In 1212 Alexander had been knighted by King John of England, but despite this honour to the heir of Scotland, relations between the two countries were deteriorating once again.

When William the Lion was old and desirous of maintaining peace even at a price, he had sent his two elder daughters to England to be married to King John's sons and had paid a joint dowry of fifteen thousand merks. King John, in possession of the two princesses, had failed to keep his part of the bargain, though he had kept the dowry. When William died and the sixteen-year-old Alexander II succeeded, King John announced in contemptuous glee that he intended to 'hunt the red fox cub from his den'.

It was small wonder that Alexander, who had the wits of a fox as well as the colouring, lent his support to the barons who forced Magna Carta on King John in 1215.

In 1221, when King John was dead, an effort was made to restore better relations, and Alexander married Joan, the daughter of John and the sister of the young King Henry III. But the loss of the fifteen thousand merks still rankled, and when Henry III was facing baronial revolt in 1232-4, Alexander demanded the return of the money, and backed his demand by reviving Scotland's claim to the lands which Malcolm IV had been forced to cede to Henry II. However, an ugly situation was composed by a meeting between the royal brothers-in-law at York in 1236, and the following year a more lasting peace was made. By the treaty of 1237 the Tweed-Solway line was agreed upon as the Border. This was by no means a final definition, for the Border was much fought over in ensuing centuries, but it sketched the line which was ultimately drawn. Alexander abandoned the old claim to the northern English counties, which he could have obtained only by conquest, and received in recompense the honour of Tynedale and the manor of Penrith, to be held of the King of England for a rent of one red falcon presented annually at the castle of Carlisle. In effect he purchased his English lands, for the disputed fifteen thousand merks was never returned. His three sisters, however, all married English noblemen, so that in the end King John's broken bargain ceased to matter.

In 1238 Alexander's English Queen died without issue, and the following year he married Marie de Coucy, the daughter of a French baron, Enguerrand de Coucy. The greatness of her family was illustrated by her father's arrogant motto :

> *Je ne suis Roy, ni Prince aussi:*
> *Je suis le Seigneur de Coucy.*

> [Though I am neither a King nor a Prince
> I am the Lord of Coucy.]

The only son of Alexander II and Queen Marie was born in 1241 and survived to reign as Alexander III.

The King's French marriage was unpopular in England, and with other causes of friction contributing, the two countries came to the brink of war. But once again diplomacy prevailed, and in 1244 it was agreed that Alexander's son should marry Henry III's daughter Margaret. The marriage took place in 1251 when the children were ten and eleven years old respectively.

In his foreign relations Alexander II's preference was for peace, though he did not hesitate to threaten war if he believed it would bring Scotland advantage. At home it was his chief desire to give his kingdom the benefits of law and order. He was successful in quelling disturbances in Moray, Caithness and Argyll. He recognized that peace in the far west could best be maintained by controlling the Western Isles, which had been officially subject to the Norwegian Crown since the reign of Edgar and unofficially since the coming of the Vikings.

Alexander first negotiated for the Isles, and when a peaceful approach failed, he resolved to attempt their conquest. However, he died suddenly in 1249, on the low green islet of Kerrera, opposite Oban, leaving the fate of the Western Isles to be decided by his son, though many years were to pass before the boy could complete what his father had begun. Alexander II, like William the Lion, had a late-born heir : he was fifty when he died, but his son was not quite eight years old.

Of his character it was said that 'he showed himself a comrade to his fellow soldiers, kindly to all religious men, humble towards the aged, and modest towards the common people; compassionate to the wretched, liberal to the poor, gentle to the just, fierce to the rebellious, terrible to wrong doers, but merciful to those who submitted.'

After his death his Queen did not remain long in Scotland, and she took little part in the upbringing of their son. In 1251 Queen Marie returned to France and married Jean de Brienne, or 'John of Acre', the son of the King of Jerusalem.

🎗 Scotland's Alexander the Great

The boy-king Alexander III was crowned at Scone and seated upon the sacred Stone. A Gaelic-speaking *seannachie*, or bard, proclaimed him 'Alexander, King of Alba, son of Alexander, son of William' and so on, back to the mythical, pre-Christian Fergus, son of Ferehard. The ceremonial common to Christian Europe blended with the ritual which survived from the Celtic past. The blending was appropriate, for in the reign of Alexander III the disparate elements of the country began to blend together as never before. The Celtic north-west and south-west of the country, and the Anglian south-east with its Norman overlay, grew to be one kingdom. Alexander III had a variety of titles – King of Alba, King of Scotia or Scotland, King of Scots – but the last (which became the preferred style of his successors) was the most appropriate, for it suggested that he was not so much a territorial ruler as the King of the various peoples who had come to regard themselves as Scots.

When Alexander was crowned, the greatness of his achievement was scarcely predictable, for he was in a dangerous position as the prospective son-in-law of an English king who concealed the rapaciousness of his desire to dominate Scotland behind a façade of fatherly concern for Alexander's welfare.

On Christmas Day 1251 Alexander was knighted by Henry III and the following day married to his daughter Margaret. Alexander did homage for his English lands and adroitly excused himself from an invitation to do homage for Scotland also.

Henry III died in 1272, and two years later Alexander III and his Queen journeyed to England to be present at the coronation of the Queen's brother Edward I. Alexander owed the new King a renewal of homage for his lands in England. He paid it with the customary reservation 'saving only for my own kingdom'. An English bishop discourteously added 'and saving the right of my lord King Edward to homage for your kindgom', to which Alexander made the courteous and unruffled response, 'to that none has a right save God alone.'

The suggestion that Alexander should pay homage for Scotland was, in twentieth-century parlance, a try-on. It was not renewed, and while Alexander III and Edward I ruled Scotland and England as brothers-in-law, friendly relations were maintained. Edward I was a realist who recognized that during the later years of Henry III, Alexander had grown into a great ruler.

In his early twenties Alexander III had set himself to complete his father's task of acquiring the Western Isles. Like his father, Alexander tried first negotiation and then conquest. In 1263 Haakon the Old, King of Norway, reluctant to lose his hold upon the Isles, brought a great fleet to Scotland, and was defeated in October at the battle of Largs. He retired to Orkney and there died. The transfer of the Isles was completed by diplomacy, and Norway ceded them to Scotland by the Treaty of Perth in 1266.

The acquisition of the Western Isles greatly enhanced Alexander's prestige, and the peace which followed enabled him to lead his kingdom towards the prosperity, order and unity which he desired. But his career provided a perfect illustration of Solon's frequently quoted saying, 'Call no man happy till he dies, at best he is but fortunate.'

Fortune, in the later years of his reign, deserted him. In 1275 his Queen died. The chronicler of Lanercost observed of her that she was 'a woman of great beauty, chastity and humility, three qualities that are seldom combined in one person'. She had borne him three children, Margaret, Alexander and David. Margaret, in pledge of peace, married Erik II of Norway in 1281, and died two years later, leaving a daughter who was also called Margaret. David died in childhood in 1281, and Alexander died at the age of twenty in 1284. The succession, which had seemed assured, was suddenly in jeopardy, represented only by the King's grand-daughter in Norway.

In 1285 Alexander married again, obviously in the hope of begetting a new family of sons. His second wife, Yolande de Dreux, was said to have been 'the fairest of women'. The marriage took place in Jedburgh Abbey on All Saints' Day, 1 November. Alexander III's biographer described the ill-omened event which took place at the wedding feast, deriving his account from the untranslated chronicle to which he refers :

> . . . In after years there was told a strange tale of a happening at that feast which men took for an omen of evil. While that noble company sat at meat there was made a masque to give them pleasure. There passed among the feasters a procession of dancers. First went the skilled musicians playing on all kinds of instruments, and after them and mingling with them in studied order a solemn dance of armed men. . . . But upon the heels of these there followed a single figure, of whom it could hardly be told whether he were a man or a phantasm. He seemed rather to glide like a shadow than pass by on his feet; and before the eyes of all the company he suddenly vanished. Then the whole gay procession was silent, as though they had seen a spirit; the singing ceased, the music was broken, and the band of dancers stood still. *Their mirth,* says the *Scotichronicon,* where the story is told, *was mingled with sorrow, and grief dashed the climax of their joy.*

Later chroniclers stated outright that Death himself had appeared at the wedding of Alexander III and Yolande de Dreux. The unknown figure, whoever he was, was recognized by posterity as a supernatural harbinger of disaster, because of the tragedy that followed.

Queen Yolande was still unpregnant when Alexander III was accidentally killed in March 1286. The King had attended a Council of his lords in Edinburgh Castle, and afterwards he dined there. Late in the evening he announced his intention of returning to Kinghorn, on the north side of the Firth of Forth, where the Queen awaited him. The night was dark and wild, but the King refused to listen to those who tried to dissuade him from setting out. With great difficulty he was ferried across the rough waters of the Forth, and on the farther shore he became separated from his two companions as they rode towards Kinghorn. Alexander was nearing his destination when his horse missed its footing on the cliff path and threw him to his death on the rocks below. The loss of the King plunged Scotland into a turmoil which prolonged the stormy darkness of that fatal night for a quarter of a century.

Alexander III's reign had in a strange manner echoed that of his father. Both father and son had been knighted by a king of England and had married an English princess; both had faced English ambition to dominate Scotland and both had frustrated it; both had been widowed of an English queen and had found a second queen in France; both had contended the sovereignty of the Western Isles with the Crown of Norway; both had died suddenly in vigorous middle age.

One of the best known pieces of medieval Scots verse laments the death of Alexander III and the passing of a period which seemed in retrospect to have been a golden age:

> When Alexander our King was dede
>   That Scotland held in love and le,*
> Away was sons† of ale and brede,
>   Of wine and wax, of game and glee,
> Our gold was changit into lede –
>   Christ, born into Virginité,
> Succour Scotland and remede
>   That stad is in perplexité.

In that verse the benefits of Alexander's reign are succinctly listed, but of all of them 'love and law' and 'game and glee' are the most worth noticing. For it is surely the ultimate test of a great ruler that his reign provides law and order maintained by love and is characterized by a joyous spirit.

℀ *The Damsel of Scotland*

King Alexander III's daughter Margaret was almost twenty when she married Erik II of Norway in 1281, but her bridegroom was only thirteen years old. Evidently the young King consummated the marriage the following year, for their child Margaret was born in April 1283.

Margaret, the little 'Maid of Norway', was thus three years

* law.   † plenty.

old when her grandfather Alexander III met his death. Though history has remembered her as 'the Maid of Norway', perhaps it would be appropriate to revive another of her titles – 'the Damsel of Scotland'.

Margaret had been recognized as heiress to the Scottish throne during her grandfather's lifetime, and the principle of primogeniture had become so firmly established that on his death she was immediately recognized as 'Lady and Queen of Scotland'. Six guardians were appointed to govern the kingdom during her minority.

Edward I, the realist who had laid no claim to the kingdom of his strong brother-in-law, saw his opportunity in the accession of a small girl. He proposed a marriage between Margaret of Scotland and his own son Prince Edward, who had been born in 1284.

By the Treaty of Salisbury of 1289 and the Treaty of Birgham of 1290 it was agreed that the Queen of Scotland should marry the heir of England. The Guardians, mindful of their duty to the kingdom, laid down conditions whereby the 'rights, laws, liberties and customs of Scotland' were to be 'wholly and inviolably preserved' and Scotland was to remain 'separate and divided from the kingdom of England'. Despite these conditions Edward I no doubt trusted that Margaret's Scotland would become subordinate to his son's England, as the wife was expected to become her husband's subordinate in marriage. However, Scotland was saved from this particular danger by the small, personal tragedy of the Queen's early death in May 1290.

Edward I had prepared a great ship to bring her from Norway. Among the provisions were figs, raisins and gingerbread. Perhaps the hard-headed King of England was capable of a kindly thought on behalf of a child; perhaps the inclusion of the medieval equivalent of sweets among the ship's stores resulted from the thoughtfulness of some lesser person. Margaret never tasted the English comfits, for her father insisted that she should sail in a Norwegian ship; but his solicitude for her welfare was in vain, for she died on the voyage, in the arms of Bishop Narve of Bergen.

The body of the Damsel of Scotland was taken back to Norway, and it was reported that King Erik 'had the coffin opened, and narrowly examined the body, and himself acknowledged that it was his daughter's corpse'.

Her brief nominal reign had a tragic but little remembered epilogue. In 1300, shortly after the death of Erik II, a young German woman from Lübeck arrived in Norway, claiming to be his daughter. She was put on trial, convicted as an impostor and burned to death in Bergen. The 'False Margaret' was surely one of the most luckless of that unhappy company of ambitious or self-deluded people who have proclaimed themselves to be of royal blood, and paid for it with their lives.

The death of the true Margaret brought the able dynasty of Dunkeld to an end. Scotland was kingless and more vulnerable to the ambitions of England than ever before.

3

THE WARS OF INDEPENDENCE
AND THE HOUSE OF BRUCE
1290-1371

🎜 The Competitors

The only way to understand what happened next in Scotland is to banish any recollection of Edward I's subsequent reputation as 'the Hammer of the Scots' and try to imagine the state of mind of the influential Scots of 1290.

With the extinction of the House of Dunkeld, the kingdom was crowded with aspirants to the throne, some of whom were prepared to fight for it. Reasonable men wish to avoid civil war, and reason prevailed.

Edward I of England had been the brother-in-law and ally of the late King Alexander, and their relationship had been that of sovereign equals; more recently Edward had been a signatory to a statesmanlike treaty which proposed that Scotland and England should be united by a marriage alliance which respected Scotland's independence. Though in the light of what happened later Edward's approach to this treaty may justly be regarded as disingenuous, in 1290 the Scots had little reason to be suspicious of him. It was reasonable that he should be requested to act as arbitrator in the succession dispute.

From that point onwards self-interest may have blinded the aspirants to some extent. By the time they realized the scope of Edward I's ambitions, their personal interests and the extent of their involvement in the arbitration prevented them from going back to the beginning again.

There were thirteen claimants to the throne. The principal claims are illustrated by Genealogical Table No 3. There were no legitimate descendants of Malcolm the Maiden or William the Lion, but these two Kings had had a younger brother, David, Earl of Huntingdon. Earl David had three daughters, Margaret, Isabella and Ada. Margaret, the eldest, married Alan, Lord of Galloway. Their daughter Devorguilla married John Balliol, a nobleman of Picard descent whose family had come to Scotland in the reign of David I; and their son, John Balliol the younger, had the best claim in strict order of primogeniture. Earl David's second daughter, Isabella, married Robert Bruce (or 'the Bruce' or 'de Brus'), Lord of Annandale, a Norman in origin, whose family also owed its advancement in Scotland to David I. The son of this marriage, also named Robert Bruce of Annandale, contested Balliol's claim on two counts : firstly, he was the grandson of Earl David, whereas Balliol was a more distant descendant as great-grandson; secondly, in 1238, while Alexander II was still childless, he had recognized Robert Bruce as his heir. The birth of Devorguilla's son had displaced Bruce as heir of line, but Alexander II's choice still arguably carried some weight. Earl David's third daughter, Ada, had married an Anglo-Norman noble named Henry de Hastings. Their grandson John, Lord Hastings, argued that David's three daughters were co-heiresses, and that Scotland was in fact a fief of England and could therefore be divided between the descendants of the heiresses : John Balliol, Robert Bruce and himself.

Hastings's argument was ingenious, but his was a forlorn hope, for a kingdom, whether it were regarded as a sovereign state or as a vassal state, was not considered divisible in the manner of an ordinary fief. There were other hopes, even more forlorn, represented by descendants of Earl David's younger sisters, descendants of Donald *Ban* in the female line and illegitimate descendants of William the Lion and Alexander II. The most ingenious outsider of all was perhaps Erik II of Norway, who claimed by ascent instead of descent, pointing out that he was the father of the late Queen Margaret.

The claimants are often referred to as the 'Competitors', a name which probably suits the mood in which they canvassed their respective claims.

Edward I requested that the competitors should acknowledge him their feudal superior, and after some hesitation they agreed to do so. His request and their response were entirely in accordance with the spirit of feudalism : he was a king and they were not, some of them indeed were his vassals already in respect of lands they held in England. Balliol and Bruce both belonged to this category. In this situation it would have been impossible for one of the competitors to stand aside from the rest without jeopardizing his chances; and neither Balliol nor Bruce, between whom the ultimate decision rested, would have been prepared to do so.

Edward I deliberated long and with every appearance of scrupulous judicial impartiality. He announced his decision in the great hall of Berwick Castle on 17 November 1292: it was an absolutely correct decision in favour of the nearest heir by primogeniture – John Balliol.

⚘ *John Balliol and Edward I*

John Balliol's contemporaries gave him the contemptuous nickname of 'Toom Tabard' (i.e. 'Empty Coat'), the implication being that he was a nonentity. Yet a stronger man than John Balliol might have found his position impossible.

Together with the rest of the competitors, Balliol had already acknowledged Edward I as his overlord. After pronouncing in Balliol's favour, Edward demanded that he should renew his oath, and Balliol was in no position to refuse. To do so would have been tantamount to reasserting the independence of Scotland, and Balliol did not command sufficient support to risk such a gesture even had he wished it. Before Edward reached his decision, the Scottish nobility had divided into Bruce and Balliol factions, and the Bruce partisans would never be loyal subjects of the new King John.

Three days after Edward's pronouncement Balliol took the renewed oath of fealty, and on the last day of November, St Andrew's Day, he was crowned at Scone. He was the last king who sat on the sacred stone where Kenneth mac Alpin had placed it. After the coronation, he followed Edward to England, and at Newcastle on 26 December he did homage for Scotland.

Once again the King of Scots was the vassal of England, but Edward was not satisfied. He had already conquered Wales, and it was soon revealed that he intended to deal likewise with Scotland.

His policy was to press his rights as Balliol's overlord to the limits of legality, until Balliol should be driven to revolt, when he could be crushed as a rebellious vassal. In so doing, while keeping technically within his rights, Edward bent the legal structure of the relationship between lord and vassal to purposes for which it had never been intended.

Balliol was summoned to do military service in France (where Edward was fighting the French King Philip IV to whom he owed homage for the English lands in France); more humiliating still, Balliol was summoned to appear in English courts to answer complaints and appeals brought by his own subjects. As Edward had intended, Balliol's authority in Scotland was undermined until his position became untenable.

John Balliol may not deserve all the contempt which has been meted out to him. His answer to Edward was not undignified. In 1295 he formally repudiated his allegiance to the English King and signed a treaty of alliance with the King of France. This treaty was the first link in the chain of treaties which bound Scotland and France together in the *auld alliance*, which endured as a political bond until the Reformation and as a tradition of friendship thereafter.

In 1296 Edward turned upon Balliol. He invaded Scotland with a great army, sacked Berwick which was then Scotland's most prosperous port, massacred the inhabitants and marched on to defeat Balliol's supporters in a battle near Dunbar. On 11 July John Balliol was forced to surrender his kingdom to Edward, and in a humiliating ceremony at Brechin the royal insignia and armorial bearings were stripped off him. Edward sent him into captivity in the Tower of London, and when he himself returned to England, he took with him the Scottish regalia and the sacred stone of Scone. A legend tells that he carried with him a substituted stone, and legend is supported by the suggestive evidence that the unimpressive block of stone now housed in Westminster Abbey has been identified by geologists as originating in the vicinity of Scone. The Stone of Destiny, even if it had never been Jacob's pillow, might have been expected to betray an origin at least as exotic as Irish Dalriada; furthermore, the stone which Edward took showed no trace of ever having borne a Latin inscription. However, the conqueror's gesture of removing it aroused sufficient resentment to invest even a debatable object with symbolic power, as recent attempts to repatriate the stone have proved. Whether it were genuine or supposititious, Edward I took a risk when he flouted the superstition concerning it; and indeed, the prophecy was eventually fulfilled when a Scottish king, James VI, sat in the Coronation Chair containing it, to be crowned as James I of England. The last that was heard of Balliol's crown was Edward's command that it should be sent to Canterbury as a shrine-offering to St Thomas Becket.

To all appearances Scotland was conquered, and Edward prepared to administer it as a province. But Edward had miscalculated when he imagined that the pathetic dignity of John Balliol was the only resistance he would encounter. The afterglow of the last Alexander's reign, the memory of a kingdom held in love and law, lived on in the minds of many Scots. Contrasted with it was the humiliation of foreign conquest, the outrage of the massacre at Berwick and the degradation of Scottish sovereignty inflicted on the person of the unfortunate Balliol. All combined to inspire a spirit of resistance as indomitable as it was unexpected.

Between 1297 and 1307 Edward I earned his title of 'the Hammer of the Scots', but his hammering served merely to forge and temper a new sense of nationhood in the kingdom which he had sought to subjugate. The resistance of Scotland during the most active period of Edward I's attempt at conquest was personified by Sir William Wallace. In September 1297 an English army commanded by the Earl of Surrey was defeated by Wallace at the battle of Stirling Bridge; but in July of the following year Wallace met defeat at the hands of Edward himself at the battle of Falkirk. After his defeat Wallace is believed to have gone abroad to seek papal support for Scotland's cause. In 1305, after his return, he was betrayed into English hands, tried and convicted of treason in Westminster Hall, and hanged, drawn and quartered at Smithfield. His execution provided Scotland's cause with a martyr. Edward's infliction of a traitor's death upon a captured enemy who had never given him allegiance was an incalculably costly error of judgment.

Edward I himself died in 1307, on the march for Scotland. He was an old man fighting a new generation of enemies, indomitable in his desire for conquest as they in theirs for freedom.

When Edward died, John Balliol was still alive. After three years in the Tower he had been allowed to retire to his estates in France. He died in 1313. Scotland and England were still at war, but the protagonists had forgotten him. Scotland, however, had not heard the last of the Balliols. By his wife, Isabella de Warenne, the daughter of the Earl of Surrey, John Balliol had a son named Edward, who many years later attempted to make good his father's claim to the Scottish throne.

🐌 *Robert the Bruce*

Edward I's last adversary was a young man who had once been high in his favour: Robert Bruce, the grandson of the Bruce who had been Balliol's nearest rival for the crown.

The early career of Robert Bruce was one of vacillation between adherence to the fealty he had sworn to Edward I and assertion of his inherited claim to the throne of Scotland. He supported Edward I when Balliol revoked his allegiance, but after Balliol's deposition he changed sides, probably with the hope of asserting his own claim. He became one of the Guardians of the resurgent Scotland, in association with John 'the Red' Comyn, Balliol's nephew. Almost immediately rivalry made them enemies. Bruce, perhaps temporarily despairing of both Scotland's cause and his own, sought a reconciliation with Edward I. But in 1305, after the death of Wallace had inflamed Scottish patriotic sentiment, he began to contemplate the great gamble of making a bid for the crown.

Early in 1306 Bruce arranged a meeting with Comyn in the Greyfriars' Church at Dumfries, possibly with the hope of composing their differences and bargaining for Comyn's support. However, old enmity reasserted itself and in the quarrel which ensued, Bruce blindly lost his temper and stabbed Comyn to death.

Comyn had lately been received into King Edward's peace, and the sacrilegious murder branded Bruce as the King of England's enemy, and put him beyond hope of another reconciliation. He had no choice but to make the great gamble which he had been cautiously contemplating, and to make it before Edward could move or the Pope put him under the ban of excommunication.

Bruce hastened to Scone with his handful of existing supporters and had himself crowned on Palm Sunday 1306. If the Stone of Destiny was still in Scotland, its whereabouts had been forgotten in the intervening time. Since he lacked the crown and the sacred stone, Bruce was seated upon a makeshift throne and crowned with a plain gold circlet. The bleak ceremony served to proclaim him; it was the long, hard years that followed which truly made him King.

At the beginning the new King Robert I was no more than a crowned fugitive, and a year of defeat and flight preceded the turn of the tide in his favour. His first victory over English forces at Loudoun Hill in 1307 stimulated the dying Edward I to lead his last invasion of Scotland.

The death of Edward I was as valuable as a second victory to King Robert, for the successor of the renowned 'Hammer of the Scots' was his imprudent and unfortunate son Edward II, the once-intended husband of the child Queen Margaret, the Damsel of Scotland.

While King Robert worked upon his twofold task of reconquering his kingdom from the English and defeating his indigenous enemies, the kindred of the murdered Comyn, Edward II, obsessed by his love for Piers Gaveston, was locked in a life and death struggle with the magnates of England, who unanimously detested the all-powerful favourite.

In 1309 King Robert held his first Parliament at St Andrews, at which he received declarations of loyalty from the clergy and nobility of Scotland. From then onwards he was able to begin clearing the English occupying forces out of the Lowlands and re-taking the strongholds from which English power had been maintained. Perth, Dumfries, Linlithgow, Roxburgh and Edinburgh fell to him. In the spring of 1314 only Stirling remained in English possession.

By this time Piers Gaveston had met his death at the hands of his enemies, and Edward II had been obliged to come to terms with them, if only in the interests of the continuity of government. He was forced to turn his attention to Scotland, and little as he cared for conquest, he realized that he must strike a blow for English prestige which had been lowered by King Robert's successes.

At midsummer 1314 Edward II led an army which probably numbered twenty thousand men to the relief of Stirling Castle, only to be devastatingly defeated at the battle of Bannockburn. It was by no means a foregone conclusion, for though Edward II was not much of a general, he had some able commanders. The credit belongs to King Robert for his generalship, and to the Scots for their unity and resolution. The Scottish army, which was about half the size of Edward's, contained a true cross-section of the nation. Bannockburn was a decisive victory, after which, in the words of a contemporary chronicler, 'Robert de Brus was commonly called King of Scotland by all men, because he had acquired Scotland by force of arms'.

Though Bannockburn was a triumph, it was not a conclusion. King Robert still faced years of struggle to win English acknowledgment of Scotland's independence, and formal recognition by the Pope, which for both political and religious reasons was essential to a Christian King.

In 1320 the Scottish nobility wrote a letter to Pope John XXII summarizing King Robert's successes and Scotland's aspirations, and requesting the recognition of their king. This letter, known as the 'Declaration of Arbroath', is regarded as Scotland's declaration of independence. It was some years before it received a satisfactory answer.

In the meantime, years of continuous warfare, which included the recapture of Berwick and two minor Scottish victories in northern England, convinced the English government of the necessity to accede to Scottish demands.

Edward II was deposed and murdered in 1327, and England was governed on behalf of the young King Edward III by his mother, Queen Isabella, and her lover, Roger Mortimer, Earl of March. To this unpopular pair belonged the opprobrium of 'losing' Scotland, although Edward I could never in truth be said to have gained it. In 1328 they negotiated with King Robert the Treaty of Northampton which acknowledged his kingship and the sovereign status of his kingdom, and promised perpetual peace between Scotland and England.

In the autumn of 1328 Pope John XXII lifted the excommunication which King Robert had incurred by his long-ago murder of Comyn. The papal missive was addressed to 'Our dearest son, Robert, Illustrious King of Scotland'. To receive those words might well have seemed to King Robert a greater victory than Bannockburn.

The following year King Robert died, having lived long enough to see the fruition of all that he had fought for; not only the recovery of Scotland's independence but the re-establishment of a kingdom in which people lived in content, under the rule of law, and had time and occasion for 'game and glee' in their lives. The prosperity which had belonged to Scotland at the end of Alexander III's reign could not indeed by regained easily. But prosperity is a god which can be too much worshipped; if terrestrial deities have to be worshipped at all, King Robert had taught his subjects to worship a better one. His credo was summed up by John Barbour, in his great epic poem *The Bruce* :

> Ah, freedom is a noble thing!
> Freedom makes man to have liking;
> Freedom all solace to man gives;
> He lives at ease that freely lives!
> A noble heart may have none ease,
> Nor anything that may him please
> If freedom fail . . . [language modernized]

King Robert had dedicated himself to ensuring that it should not fail. Since he was a hero to his people, in the manner of heroes he became part of folklore as well as part of history. His minor exploits, true and apocryphal, were remembered perhaps better than some of his more important achievements: how he learned the lesson of perseverance from a spider; how he kept up the courage of his fugitive companions by reading aloud to them a romance of chivalry; how he drew first blood at the battle of Bannockburn by slaying Sir Henry de Bohun in single combat.

Before his death King Robert requested that his heart should be carried into battle against the enemies of Christ, for life had never allowed him time to fulfil the medieval ideal of going on crusade. The King's faithful supporter Sir James Douglas obeyed his last wish and took the King's heart to Spain, where he carried it with him into battle against the Moors. Douglas was killed near Granada in 1330, and the following year the King's heart was brought back to Scotland by Sir William Keith and buried in the abbey of Melrose. His body was buried in Dunfermline.

King Robert was twice married. By his first wife, Isabella of Mar, he had a daughter named Margery, who married Walter Stewart, sixth hereditary High Steward of Scotland. Their son eventually became Robert II, the first King of the House of Stewart. By his second wife, Elizabeth de Burgh, King Robert had a son born in 1324, who in the meantime, at the age of five, succeeded as David II.

🌺 *David II*

The small King of Scots was already married. As the pledge of peace with England he had been married at the age of four to Joan of the Tower, the younger daughter of Edward II. Andrew of Wyntoun wrote a charming description of her:

> Sche was sweet and debonair,
> Curteis, hamelie, pleasand and fair.

King Robert I had won from the Pope the privilege of anointing for future Kings of Scots, for the sacred rite would enhance their prestige and remove any lingering impression that Scottish kings were inferior to English kings, who were customarily anointed. In accordance with the papal concession, David II became Scotland's first anointed king when he received the holy oil at his coronation in 1331.

Despite the apparently secure condition in which King Robert had left his kingdom, the minority of David II was a troubled time. The reason was not far to seek : while Scotland was at a disadvantage with a boy King under the tutelage of a series of regents, England had a strong and militaristic King again.

Edward III had resented the Treaty of Northampton, which he regarded as a betrayal of his grandfather's achievements. In 1330 he overthrew the authority of his mother and Mortimer and quickly showed that he did not intend to be bound by the peace which they had made with Scotland.

In character Edward III was very much his grandfather's grandson, and history repeated itself to the extent that in Edward Balliol, the son of the erstwhile King John, he found a man who was eager to become King of Scots on the same terms, as a vassal of England.

Edward Balliol invaded Scotland with English support and with that of 'the Disinherited' – certain Scottish lords who had been deprived of their lands in Scotland by King Robert when they chose the English side in the first War of Independence. Edward Balliol and his supporters defeated the forces of David II in August 1332, at the battle of Dupplin Moor, near Perth. The following month Edward Balliol was crowned at Scone, but the supporters of David rallied and drove him out of Scotland before the end of the year. He fled the country ignominiously, riding bareback with 'one leg booted and the other naked'.

Edward III came to his aid, and in July 1333 their combined forces defeated the young King of Scots at Halidon Hill, near Berwick. The situation of Scotland seemed as desperate as it had been in the days of Edward I. King David and his child-Queen were sent to France for safety, while the King's loyal supporters fought a second War of Independence with all the tenacity that Sir William Wallace and King Robert I had shown in the early years of the century.

K. & Q.—3

A leading part in the renewed struggle was taken by Robert Stewart, the grandson of King Robert I and the heir presumptive to the crown, who was eight years older than his uncle King David.

Slowly the tide turned against Edward Balliol. Edward III's attention was distracted from Scotland by the larger scope of his ambitions in France. He had a specious claim to the French throne through his mother, Queen Isabella, who had been a French princess. Edward III's determination to make good his claim involved England in the Hundred Years' War with France and saved Scotland's independence a second time.

In 1341 it was considered safe for King David and his Queen to return to Scotland. However, it was not long before David was called upon to repay the hospitality he had received in France. In August 1346 Edward III inflicted a heavy defeat on the French at the battle of Crècy, and David, in accordance with the terms of the Franco-Scottish alliance, invaded northern England and was defeated and captured at the battle of Neville's Cross, near Durham, in October.

Robert Stewart, who had commanded the left wing of the army, withdrew his troops in good order, and King David, who remained a prisoner in England for the next eleven years, had ample opportunity to brood upon the question of whether his heir presumptive had treacherously deserted him, or not. From 1346 to 1357 Robert acted as Regent or Guardian of the Kingdom, and King David's view of him grew less than charitable.

David II, although a prisoner, lived at the English Court as an honoured guest. Both during and after his captivity he cultivated an apparently close though not necessarily sincere friendship with Edward III. A fourteenth-century illuminated miniature provides a vignette of this curious relationship: King Edward gazes with brooding intensity at King David who, standing ingratiatingly at his side, shakes him warmly by the hand. Eventually David was ransomed for the huge sum of a hundred thousand merks, which was to be paid in ten instalments.

It was in the years after his return from captivity, when

Scotland truly came to know him, that his reputation was inevitably made or marred. Perhaps it was not surprising that he gained a poor reputation, for he had the unenviable inheritance of a legendary father. David II was not cast in a heroic mould, and his one attempt to act heroically bore the bitter fruit of captivity. Yet when he returned to Scotland, chastened and matured, he proved to be an astute and patient man, and not altogether an unsuccessful king. His long absence had invited disorder, but gradually his grip on the kingdom tightened until towards the end of his reign it was said that 'nane durst well wythstand his will'. Furthermore, Scotland began to prosper again, despite two visitations of the Black Death – 'the foul death of the English', as the Scots called it – in 1349–50 and in 1361–2.

David II's Queen had lived with him in England throughout his captivity, but no child was born to them. Understandably David did not view the succession of Robert Stewart with much favour. He seems to have preferred the prospect of succession by one of the sons of Edward III should he himself die without issue; on the other hand, the collection of the ransom payments demanded the imposition of heavy taxation upon his subjects, and he bargained the proposed English succession against the remission of the balance of his ransom. At the same time he did not give up hope of foiling the ambitions of both Robert Stewart and Edward III by begetting a son.

In 1362 Queen Joan died still childless, and in the spring of 1363 David married his mistress, Dame Margaret Logie, the daughter of Sir Malcolm Drummond. Dame Margaret had a child by her first marriage, but she failed to bear a child to King David. In 1370 he divorced her and announced his intention of marrying a lady named Agnes Dunbar.

Margaret, however, was not to be disposed of so easily. She journeyed to Avignon to appeal at the papal court against the divorce which had taken place in Scotland, and the Pope reversed the decision of the Scottish bishops. King David's matrimonial problems were still unresolved when he died suddenly in February 1371, at the age of forty-six.

The Scottish Parliament had repudiated his proposal for the

succession of an English prince and stated its preference for the heir presumptive. The Parliament had now come to consist of the 'Three Estates' of the realm – nobility, clergy and commons. The commons, as representative of the prosperous burghs, had been summoned to Parliament in the first place that they might contribute to the taxation imposed to collect the King's ransom. But to all three estates the dearly bought independence of the kingdom seemed more desirable than the financial benefit of a close link with England, which, despite constitutional safe-guards, would certainly jeopardize independence once again.

David II has often been accused of readiness to betray his father's ideals. Perhaps he should be given the benefit of the doubt for his delicate and dangerous diplomacy which was prob-ably intended to fill in time until he should produce an heir.

Since he died childless, the short-lived House of Bruce died with him. His successor, Robert II, whom David had viewed with suspicion and dislike, was at least a man who could be trusted never to betray the best interests of the kingdom.

4

THE HOUSE OF STEWART

1371–1603

✿ From Stewardship to Kingship

The very existence of the first Stewart King was something of a miracle, for he had been delivered by caesarian section from the body of Margery Bruce, who died in childbirth after a fall from her horse.

Robert Stewart was born in February 1316. Two years later he was recognized as the heir of his grandfather, a position from which he was demoted by the birth of the future David II in 1324. Forty-seven years later, when David II against all likelihood and expectation had failed to perpetuate his dynasty, Robert was crowned at Scone, on 22 February 1371.

It was from Margery Bruce that King Robert II derived his royal blood and his claim to the throne. His paternal ancestry was not dissimilar to that of the Bruces and the Balliols, for his father's family, like theirs, owed its establishment in Scotland to David I.

The first recorded ancestor of the Stewarts was a nobly born Breton named Alan, who was *dapifer* or steward to the Count of Dol in the late eleventh century. It is worth remembering that while the Balliols and the Bruces were of Picard and Norman origin respectively, the Stewarts, being of Breton and therefore Celtic stock, were ethnically more akin to the majority of their subjects than any king of Scots had been since the last of the House of Dunkeld.

Alan the *dapifer* had a son named Flaald who sought advancement in Britain, where he held land on the Welsh Marches in the reign of Henry I. Flaald's grandson Walter won the favour of David I, who granted him the barony of Renfrew and appointed him High Steward of Scotland. The office became hereditary in the family, whence derived the surname of Stewart. From the twelfth century the family of the High Stewards was among the greatest of the Scottish nobility, and Sir Walter Stewart, the admired young knight who was the sixth holder of the hereditary office, was considered a worthy match for the daughter of King Robert I.

When their son, at the age of fifty-four, became King Robert II, the problem of securing the succession was uppermost in his mind. In contrast with David II, he was plentifully endowed with children. He had six sons and seven daughters by his two marriages. In addition he had eight illegitimate sons, giving him a total of twenty-one children. It appeared that the succession was amply assured; the problem consisted in whether or not his first family was legitimate.

Robert's first wife was Elizabeth Mure of Rowallan, to whom he was related within the 'forbidden degrees' of kinship, which meant that he required a papal dispensation to marry her. As the forbidden degrees were remarkably ramifying, Robert and his wife may not at first have known that their relationship was within them, for it was some years before they applied for the dispensation, and the children who had already been born to them were technically illegitimate. Whether or not the dispensation subsequently granted served to legitimatize them was arguable. After Elizabeth Mure's death, Robert married as his second wife Euphemia of Ross, and the legitimacy of his second family was beyond question.

Robert II took his stand upon the efficacy of the dispensation, and by an act of succession of 1373 it was declared that the crown should go to his eldest son, John, Earl of Carrick and his heirs male, whom failing to the next son and his heirs male, and so on throughout the sons of his first and second marriages. The family of Euphemia of Ross, however, remained convinced of the superiority of its claim, eventually to the extent of committing murder for it.

Robert II triumphed in his determination to secure the rights of his eldest son, but he had few other successes to his credit. The youthful vigour which had enabled him to fight for the independence of the kingdom, to rule competently as regent and to beget many children, had deserted him by the time he became King. Furthermore, he was troubled by a complaint which caused him to have 'red bleared eyes the colour of sandalwood, which showed him to be no valiant man, but one who would rather remain at home than march to the field'. The latter part of that rather unfeeling description had certainly not always been true of him.

When Robert II came to the throne, a fourteen years' truce with England still had twelve years to run, but unofficial warfare on the Border continued in spite of it. Full-scale war broke out again in 1385 as a by-product of the Hundred Years' War between England and France. A French expeditionary force was sent to Scotland, which in turn provoked an English invasion led by Richard II, who burned the Scottish Border abbeys.

King Robert played no part in these events, and his control of internal affairs progressively weakened. In 1384 he appointed his heir, John, Earl of Carrick, to enforce authority on his behalf, but Carrick was scarcely more effective than his father, and the disorder of the kingdom increased during the last years of the reign.

In 1390 Robert II died at the age of seventy-four, and one frail and ageing king was succeeded by another : the Earl of Carrick was already about fifty-three, and two years previously he had been kicked by a horse and had sustained an injury from which he never fully recovered.

🦡 Robert III and Robert, Duke of Albany

The new King's invalidism was not his only disability. Contemporary superstition did not favour his Christian name, for King John of Scotland had been the vassal of Edward I, King John of England had been compelled to become the vassal of the Pope, and King John of France had been captured by the English at the battle of Poitiers. John of Carrick attempted to avert the omens by assuming the style of Robert III. He was so far successful as to avoid the forms of misfortune which had befallen the other kings named John, but he could not avert the consequences of his personal weakness.

Robert III delegated his authority to his next brother, Robert, Earl of Fife, who was a man of ruthless ambition; but Fife was

more concerned with his own advancement than with the welfare
of the kingdom, and internal disorder increased. The condition
of Scotland during the last years of the fourteenth century was
summed up by the chronicler who wrote : 'In those days there
was no law in Scotland, but he who was stronger oppressed
him who was weaker, and the whole kingdom was a den of
thieves'.

In 1393 King Robert, evidently dissatisfied with the efforts of
his brother, decided to resume his responsibilities, and for the
next six years he vainly attempted to keep order in his kingdom.
Doubtless it was in despair at his failure that Robert III told his
Queen, Annabella Drummond, that she need give him no epitaph
but 'Here lies the worst of Kings and the most miserable of men'.
The Queen to whom he spoke this in his bitterness of spirit died
in 1401; it was after her death that he had to endure the worst of
his miseries.

By Queen Annabella the King had two surviving sons, named
David and James. In 1399 he delegated his authority to his elder
son, whom he created Duke of Rothesay. The Earl of Fife, who
had expected a second spell in office as his brother's deputy, was
compensated with the title of Duke of Albany.

The King had made an unhappy decision, for Rothesay was a
wild and irresponsible young man, and Albany was coldly determined to oust him from office and to rule in his place. In 1401
Rothesay, who had proved himself incompetent to govern,
refused to resign his office when required to do so, and his father
was persuaded to order his arrest. He was placed in Albany's
custody, in the castle of Falkland, where he died in 1402.

Inevitably, and perhaps with justice, Albany was suspected of
having caused his death. Sinister rumours circulated that
Rothesay had died of starvation, but Albany was too powerful
to be brought to book. Though he faced a judicial enquiry, he
was predictably exonerated.

Robert III seems to have been unwilling to suspect his
brother. Yet perhaps doubts of Albany's innocence grew gradually in his mind and he began to fear what might befall his
younger son, Prince James, if he himself should die leaving the

boy in Albany's power. In 1406 he decided that James should be sent to the safety of France, and in March the eleven-year-old Prince put to sea in a ship of Danzig named the *Maryenknycht*.

It seemed as though an adverse fate waited upon the King's decisions. The ship was captured by English pirates, and the Scottish Prince was sent as a captive to the Court of Henry IV, the Lancastrian usurper who had seized the throne of Richard II. Although a truce was in force between Scotland and England, Henry did not hesitate to keep his prisoner. James remained in English captivity for eighteen years.

King Robert III died on 4 April 1406, probably on receiving the news of his son's capture. He was aged about sixty-nine and enfeebled beyond his years.

Parliament at once acknowledged the captive Prince as King of Scots, but the Duke of Albany became King in all but name. He assumed the title 'Governor of Scotland', and the documents which were issued under the great seal which showed him enthroned like a king were dated in the year of his governorship and not of the reign.

Albany ruled from 1406 to 1420. Though he possessed more astuteness than either Robert II or Robert III, he lacked the authority, and possibly the will, to restore order in Scotland. His policy was survival in office for himself and the transferring of the crown from the captive King to his own family. As a first step in this direction, Albany ransomed his son Murdoch Stewart, who had been a prisoner in England since 1402 when he was captured at the battle of Homildon, where the Scots suffered a defeat at English hands. After his return to Scotland, Murdoch was associated with his father in the government, while the King remained unransomed.

When Albany died at the age of about eighty, Murdoch succeeded him as Governor. The King's situation might have been desperate had Murdoch been a man of any ability, but his attempt at government foundered after four years of futile misrule. The King returned to a kingdom which sorely needed him, in 1424.

🎗 *James I: Poet and Lawgiver*

From the age of eleven to the age of twenty-nine King James I
had lived in England, sometimes a prisoner in the Tower or
some other royal stronghold, sometimes a participant in the life
of the Court.

James grew to be an athletic young man who delighted in
martial sports – jousting, swordsmanship and archery – and in
wrestling and throwing the hammer. Probably because the
restraint upon his liberty did not allow sufficient outlet for his
vigour, he turned his frustrated energies to the things of the
mind. He became a good linguist, musician and singer – 'another
Orpheus' according to a contemporary opinion – and a distinguished poet.

In the last year of his captivity, 1423, occurred the romantic
experience which inspired his famous poem *The Kingis Quair*
(i.e. *The King's Book*). It was probably at Windsor that James,
looking from his window in the early morning, saw a lady walk-
ing in the garden below and fell in love with her at first sight. In
his own words:

> *And therewith kest I doune myn eye ageyne,*
> *Quare as I saw, walking under the toure,*
> *Full secretly new cummyn hir to pleyne,*
> *The fairest or the freschest younge floure*
> *That evir I saw, me thoght, before that houre,*
> *For which sodayn abate, anon astert*
> *The blude of all my bodye to my hert. . . .*

She proved to be Lady Joan Beaufort, a great-grand-daughter of
Edward III. Seldom were passion and policy more fortunately
blended, for by birth she was suited to be James's Queen, and he
fell in love with her at the time when the first serious negotiations for his release had begun.

James's captivity had endured throughout the last seven years
of the reign of Henry IV and the entire reign of Henry V. The
regents for the infant Henry VI, faced with the difficulties of

holding Henry v's conquests in France, were eager to negotiate the release of the King of Scots, one of the conditions being that no more Scots would be permitted to fight for the French. How valuable this agreement would be to England is illustrated by the fact that Albany's younger son was Constable of France, and other noblemen and many thousands of Scottish soldiers were in French service. At the same time Murdoch, whose authority was flouted throughout Scotland, was willing to accept the return of the King. A ransom of sixty thousand merks, tactfully described as the King's expenses in England, was agreed upon. James married Lady Joan Beaufort in the Thames-side church which is now Southwark Cathedral, and in the spring of 1424 the King and Queen rode northward to their kingdom.

James I faced the task of ruling with determination rather than with optimism. When he discovered the full extent of the disorder in Scotland, his resolute comment was, 'If God grant me life, though it be but the life of a dog, there shall be no place in my realm where the key shall not keep the castle and the bracken bush the cow.' The story of the rest of his life is the story of how he put those words into effect.

Since his kingship had been at risk while he was in England, James I did not intend that it should be threatened after his return to Scotland. In 1425 Murdoch and his two sons were executed, and two descendants of Euphemia of Ross, the Earl of Strathearn and James, Master of Atholl (see Genealogical Table No 4), were sent to England as hostages for the payment of the King's ransom.

James turned his attention to the condition of the kingdom. His first legislation made provision for keeping 'firm and sure peace' throughout the country. The underlying purposes of all his enactments were the punishment of rebels and all other evildoers, the prevention of crime, the defence of the ordinary people who for the last fifty years had suffered most from the lawless condition of Scotland, and the building up of the royal finances which provided the means of government.

He endeavoured to improve the quality of both civil and criminal justice, and in 1426 he founded a new court, later known as 'the Session', which consisted of the Chancellor and 'certain discreet persons of the Three Estates', the purpose of which was to hear the cases previously brought before the King in Council or before Parliament. It was to James's lasting credit that he provided a 'poor man's advocate' whose services should be available to 'any poor creature' who could not pay for his own defence.

Gradually James I made Scotland fit to live in once again, as it had scarcely been since the last years of David II. Perth became his favoured place of residence, almost his capital, for its position enabled him to direct his attention equally to the Highlands and the Lowlands. The Lord of the Isles, the most wayward magnate of the north-west, suffered a severe defeat at the hands of James I in 1429; but the King realized that in the long run patient administration would achieve far more than sporadic military ventures. If the exigencies of Anglo-Scottish relations had not ultimately fixed the capital at Edinburgh, the Highlands might greatly have benefited from a more northerly centre of government.

It was at Perth that James I met his death, in February 1437, when he fell victim to a conspiracy to put Walter, Earl of Atholl, the younger son of Euphemia of Ross, on the throne. Atholl had been loyal while his son, the Master, was a hostage in England, but after his son died there, he felt the stirrings of ambition on behalf of himself and his grandson Robert, Master of Atholl, whose loyalty the King does not seem to have suspected. Inspired and abetted by Sir Robert Graham, an uncle of the Earl of Strathearn, who was still in England, Atholl plotted the murder of the King.

On the night of 20 February 1437, the conspirators forced their way into the Dominican Priory at Perth, where the King had spent the Christmas Season, and stabbed him to death in a vault beneath his bedchamber where he tried to take refuge. The Queen was wounded in attempting to defend him.

Though the King was killed, the conspiracy failed in its ultimate purpose, for James I was survived and succeeded by his six-year-old son. The conspirators, who had expected a popular rising in support of Atholl's claim, were disappointed, for the people of Scotland had forgotten Elizabeth Mure and Euphemia of Ross, and thought only of an admired *'legifer Rex'* whose son was the rightful King.

Queen Joan, James's 'freshest young flower', is said to have been responsible for the unprecedented refinements of torture with which the Earl of Atholl, the Master of Atholl and Sir Robert Graham met their death in Edinburgh, before the eyes of a gratified populace.

In 1439 the widowed Queen Joan married Sir James Stewart, 'the Black Knight of Lorne', to whom she bore three sons : John, Earl of Atholl; James, Earl of Buchan; and Andrew, Bishop of Moray. Queen Joan died in 1445 and was buried beside James I in the Church of the Charterhouse of Perth.

🙊 *James II: 'James of the Fiery Face'*

James II was the survivor of twin sons born to Queen Joan in October 1430. The tradition which originated with Kenneth mac Alpin was broken when he was crowned not at Scone but in the Abbey of Holyrood.

François Villon, in his *Ballade des Seigneurs de Temps Jadis*, described James II as having half his face the colour of an amethyst from the forehead to the chin. The King's nickname of 'James of the Fiery Face', and the visual evidence of a contemporary drawing, both substantiate the description.

Perhaps the psychological effect of such a disfigurement should not be underestimated. No doubt on public occasions the half-purple face would have seemed the more unhappily conspicuous. Not surprisingly, James II became a king who had little liking for ceremonial, a soldierly king, swift and ruthless in his dealings with adversaries.

At the beginning of his minority the Governor of the Realm was the fifth Earl of Douglas, whose mother was a daughter of Robert III. Douglas proved an ineffectual governor, and the King's childhood was dominated by a bitter power struggle between two lesser men, Sir William Crichton, the governor of Edinburgh Castle, and Sir Alexander Livingstone, the governor of Stirling Castle, each of whom in turn gained power by securing the King's person.

The governor of the realm died in 1439, and the following year Crichton and Livingstone joined forces to destroy his ambitious son William, sixth Earl of Douglas, and the latter's brother, who were invited to Edinburgh Castle and there treacherously seized at the 'Black Dinner' on 24 November 1440, and executed before the eyes of the ten-year-old King. The seventh Earl of Douglas, James 'the Gross', was the great-uncle of the murdered youths, and he was suspected of having been accessory to the crime. James the Gross and the Livingstone family gradually gained power at Crichton's expense, and for the rest of the minority the Douglas-Livingstone interest was paramount in Scotland.

In 1449 James II, at the age of nineteen, married Marie of Gueldres, the devout and civilized niece of Philip 'the Good', Duke of Burgundy. Shortly afterwards James, probably encouraged by his Queen, asserted his own authority. The Livingstones fell from power, and two members of the family were executed. The King had a harder task to overthrow the Douglases, now headed by William, the eighth Earl, eldest son of James the Gross.

The young Earl possessed immense estates in the south-west of Scotland and in the Borders, a tapering triangle of territory, which at its broad end took in the whole of Galloway and at its narrow end extended as far as Jedburgh. His ambition seems to have been to attain a position like that of the Dukes of Brittany and Burgundy in relation to the Crown of France : a position of practical independence which would permit him to ally himself with the King of Scots or with foreign powers, as best suited his interests.

James II was determined to reduce Douglas to the condition of a subject, and the climax of the struggle was reached in 1452, when the King discovered that the Earl was engaged in treasonable dealings with England and had formed a potentially traitorous alliance with the Lord of the Isles and the Earl of Crawford. James II summoned Douglas to Stirling, revealed his knowledge of the Earl's treason and desired him to repudiate his allies and reaffirm his allegiance. Douglas refused, a violent quarrel ensued and James lost his temper and stabbed the Earl to death. It was an event which strangely echoed Robert I's murder of 'the Red' Comyn, and like that earlier murder it led to war.

In a trial of strength the King had the advantage, for he was an enthusiast for the new military science of gunnery, and he possessed massive bronze cannon which enabled him to batter down the walls of the Douglas strongholds. The great gun 'Mons Meg', still to be seen in Edinburgh Castle, was cast for James II. The Douglases were finally defeated in 1455 at the battle of Arkinholm. James, ninth Earl, the next brother of the Earl whom the King had murdered, fled to England; two more of his brothers died in the same year, one killed at Arkinholm and the other captured and executed.

James II's triumph in Scotland coincided with the outbreak of the Wars of the Roses in England. The fugitive Earl of Douglas joined his forces to the House of York, while James II allied himself with Henry VI, the last King of the House of Lancaster. Scotland was more fortunate than England in the second half of the fifteenth century, for while the weakness of Henry VI plunged England into sanguinary chaos, the vigour of James II rescued Scotland from the threat of similar conflict and restored law and order.

In his fairly brief personal reign, James II showed himself a worthy successor of his father. The Parliament of 1458 congratulated him on the extent to which he had re-established the rule of law in Scotland and entreated him to continue his good work, 'that God may be empleased of him and all his lieges may pray for him to God and give thanks to Him that sends them such a Prince to be their governor and defender'.

The King was given little time in which to respond to this encouragement. In 1460 war broke out again after James had objected to Yorkist patronage of the Earl of Douglas. It was ostensibly as the ally of Henry VI that James went to war, but he endeavoured to take advantage of English civil strife by laying siege to Roxburgh Castle which was held by a Yorkist governor. The Scottish fortress had been in English hands since the reign of David II, and James II saw his way to recover it and to strike a blow for his ally Henry VI simultaneously.

It was the King's enthusiasm for gunnery which led to his accidental death at the siege of Roxburgh, on 3 August 1460. He was personally supervising the firing of one of his cannon, which had been over-generously charged with gunpower. The cannon burst and the King was instantaneously killed.

🐉 James III: *Patron of the Arts*

As soon as the Queen, Marie of Gueldres, received the news of her husband's death, she hastened to Roxburgh, taking with her their eldest son, James, who was nine years old. She urged the commanders of the army to make James II's death remembered as an occasion of victory, and they responded to her words by successfully storming Roxburgh within a few days. With his reign inaugurated by a victory, the new King James III was crowned in the nearby Abbey of Kelso on 10 August 1460.

Scotland once again faced the problems of a royal minority. Early in the new reign the kingdom was threatened by a treaty between the new King of England – the successful Yorkist claimant Edward IV – the exiled Earl of Douglas and the Lord of the Isles, whereby the two Scottish signatories were to partition Scotland and rule as vassals of England. James III's government circumvented the danger by abandoning the Lancastrian interest and making a long-term truce with Edward IV. Foreign relations, however, did not constitute Scotland's only problem. The conditions of a minority offered tacit encouragement to ambitious men, especially after the deaths of Marie of Gueldres in 1463 and the King's wise mentor Bishop Kennedy of St Andrews in 1465. The following year the King was seized at Linlithgow and carried off to Edinburgh by Lord Boyd of Kilmarnock and his brother Sir Alexander Boyd, who was the King's military tutor and the governor of Edinburgh Castle. James III was forced to make a public declaration of his approval of the *coup d'état*, and for the rest of the minority the Boyds enjoyed supreme power. The pattern of James II's minority was repeating itself.

The Boyds endeavoured to secure themselves by marrying Lord Boyd's son to the King's sister Princess Mary. An advantageous marriage was also arranged for the King. In 1469, when James III was eighteen years old, he married Margaret of Denmark, the daughter of King Christian I of Denmark, Norway and Sweden. Margaret's father pledged the estates of the Norwegian Crown in Orkney and Shetland against the payment of his daughter's dowry, and since he failed to raise the agreed sum, the Northern Isles became subject to the Scottish Crown. They were formally annexed to Scotland in 1472.

James III imitated his father in asserting his authority shortly after his marriage; the Boyds, like the Livingstones in the previous reign, paid the penalty for their presumption. Sir Alexander Boyd was executed, and Lord Boyd and his son both fled the country and died in exile.

In Margaret of Denmark, who was only thirteen at the time of her marriage, Scotland almost acquired a second St Margaret, for after her death in 1486 James III petitioned Pope Innocent VIII for her canonization. Margaret of Denmark was devout and charitable, and according to a chronicler of the next generation, she possessed kindness, gentleness and 'charm of spirit'. She offered exemplary devotion to her complicated and difficult husband, to whom she bore three sons.

James III was a young man of unusual beauty, whose dark eyes, black hair and olive skin gave him a foreign appearance. He may have resembled his mother in looks as he did in character, for he inherited Queen Marie's piety and the appreciation of the arts which she had derived from her upbringing at the Court of Burgundy.

James was a lavish and discerning patron of the arts, whose chief loves were music and architecture. He was evidently informed of European developments in painting, for he commissioned from Hugo van der Goes an altarpiece of which surviving panels contain portraits of him and his Queen. He collected classical manuscripts; he encouraged the Scottish Renaissance poets whose finest work belongs to his reign and to the next; he was responsible for a beautiful coinage which is believed to bear the first Renaissance coin-portrait produced outside Italy; and, to judge from an inventory of his possessions, he had a great love for the elaborate jewellery which was characteristic of the period.

James III was isolated from the majority of his nobility by his esoteric tastes. Furthermore, as a lover of peace in a militaristic age, he made no secret of his contempt for violence and his lack of interest in the martial pastimes in which medieval and Renaissance kings were expected to excel. He gathered around himself a coterie of favourites, some of whom could claim distinction in the arts, some of whom apparently could not. His chief favourite was Robert Cochrane, the architect of the great hall of Stirling Castle, a talented but overbearing man who made himself universally unpopular.

It is probable that James III's addiction to his favourites carried more than a suspicion of homosexuality, for prejudice against it provides the most convincing explanation of the savagery with which Cochrane and some of the others were done to death later in the reign. The parallel of Edward II and Piers Gaveston is immediately obvious.

James III's troubles began when his younger brothers Alexander, Duke of Albany, and John, Earl of Mar, reached adulthood. Both were normal, warlike young men, and Albany, like his namesake the Governor of Scotland, aspired to the throne. In 1479 both Albany and Mar were arrested upon suspicion of treasonable plotting against the King. Mar died in prison, but Albany escaped to pursue his ambitions abroad. He first tried France, where King Louis XI arranged an aristocratic marriage for him but refused to help him supplant his brother. Albany then went to England where he found a more encouraging patron in Edward IV. Relations between Scotland and England had recently deteriorated, and Edward IV was tempted by Albany to revive the English claim to overlordship of Scotland. On 10 June 1482 Edward recognized Albany as 'Alexander IV' of Scotland. An army commanded by Edward's brother Richard, Duke of Gloucester, was provided for him, and

Albany and Gloucester invaded Scotland to install 'Alexander IV' as a vassal king.

James III responded to the challenge and marched south to meet his brother. Unwisely he appointed Cochrane Master of the Artillery and went to war accompanied by all his favourites. The extent of Albany's treason was not yet known in Scotland, and his previous imprisonment had won him the sympathy of the Scottish nobility. The lords who had been summoned to follow James experienced a revulsion of feeling against the King and his favourites. When the royal army encamped at Lauder, a group of noblemen, headed by the fifth Earl of Angus, seized Cochrane and five others and hanged them over Lauder Bridge. The King was forced to witness the massacre before he was escorted back to Edinburgh as a prisoner.

Albany, however, arrived in Edinburgh to a reception very different from his expectation. The lords refused to countenance the deposition of James, probably upon the discovery of Albany's traitorous agreement with Edward IV. Albany was obliged to compose his differences with his brother, and Gloucester retired to England. Edward IV's only gain was the town of Berwick, which Gloucester had taken with Albany's assistance.

James III recovered his position and endeavoured to win Albany's loyalty by granting him a measure of power as Lieutenant of the Kingdom. The experiment was a failure, and early in 1483 Albany was again discovered in treasonable intrigues. He fled to England, only to learn that Edward IV was dead. Gloucester, who usurped the English throne as Richard III, spent his short reign struggling to retain his sovereignty and had no attention to spare for Albany. In 1484 Albany made a last attempt to seize his brother's throne when he invaded Scotland with the long-exiled Earl of Douglas. They were defeated at Lochmaben, and Douglas was captured and imprisoned. Albany fled to France where he was killed at a tournament the following year.

It seemed that James III's troubles were at an end. Though he was reproached for neglecting the routine of government, he was a patient and astute diplomatist, whose consistent purpose of keeping the peace between Scotland and England ought to

receive more credit than is generally accorded it. His final
achievement was a treaty of 1487 with Richard III's supplanter,
Henry VII, the first Tudor King of England. Henry VII married
Edward IV's daughter, Elizabeth of York, and it was agreed that
James III's eldest son, Prince James, should marry one of her
sisters, and that James III himself, now a widower, should marry
Edward IV's widow, Queen Elizabeth Woodville. The projected
double link between the royal Houses would have secured the
peace between the two kingdoms in a manner which permitted
no threat to Scotland's independence. The marriage treaty was
accompanied by preliminary negotiations for the return of
Berwick to Scotland.

James III's hopeful diplomacy came to nothing when his personal unpopularity brought about the crisis of the reign. After
his recovery of power in 1482, James had made no concessions
to public opinion in the matter of his favourites. Cochrane's
place in his affections was taken by John Ramsay of Balmain, a
young man of good family, unconnected with the arts, whom he
created Earl of Bothwell. The political influence permitted to the
favourite may once again have presented the more conservative
of the nobility with a situation which appeared intolerable.

A powerful opposition group, again headed by the Earl of
Angus, seized the fifteen-year-old Prince James, who was old
enough to be an effective figurehead but not old enough to resist
manipulation. James III gathered a by no means negligible army
of supporters, and on 11 June 1488 the reluctant son and equally
reluctant father faced each other in battle, on the field of
Sauchieburn, near Stirling.

Victory went to the rebels, and James III was urged to flee.
According to the traditional account, written in the next century,
he was thrown from his horse and injured. Rescued by the miller
of Bannockburn and his wife, he was carried into the mill, where
he asked for the services of a priest. The miller's wife went to
seek for one and returned with a stranger who promised to hear
the King's confession. The stranger, whose sympathy lay with
the rebels, gave the King no absolution but stabbed him to death
and then fled, unidentified and unscathed.

James III was buried with all solemnity, beside Margaret of Denmark, in the Abbey of Cambuskenneth. His subjects consigned an intelligent but unpopular King to oblivion and turned their attention to his son.

James IV: Once and Future King

Although the young James IV was not responsible for his father's death, he was oppressed by the guilt of his involvement with it. He chose, as a self-imposed penance, to wear an iron chain round his waist for the rest of his life; as the years passed, extra links were forged to add to its weight, so that the weight upon his conscience should never grow less.

The circumstances which had made him King brought James IV to early maturity. He rapidly became a strong and able ruler, a man of immense vigour, intelligence and vision, admired for his kingly qualities and beloved for his humanity and his informal warmth. His accomplishments were varied and impressive: he spoke eight languages including Gaelic; he appreciated learning and the arts to an extent which made him a knowledgable patron yet did not make him seem, like his father, inaccessibly intellectual; he was a superb horseman, he delighted in hunting and excelled at martial sports. James IV was susceptible to women. The Court poet William Dunbar wrote a good-humouredly satirical account of one of his seductions, in which the King is represented as a fox and his mistress as a lamb:

> *The tod was nather lene nor skowry,*
> *He wes ane lusty reid-haired lowry.*
> *Ane lang taild beist and grit withal;*
> *The silly lame wes all to small*
> *To sic ane tribill to hald ane bace:*
> *Scho feld him nocht; fair mot hir fall!*
> *And that me thocht ane ferly cace.*

[Author's translation:

> The fox was neither ragged nor lean
> A lustier reynard was never seen:

He was long tailed and large withal.
The silly ewe-lamb was much too small
To answer 'no' when he said 'yea'.
Good luck to her, whatever befall!
She didn't flee him, strange to say.]

James IV had five children by his four mistresses, and he provided for them royally. His eldest illegitimate son, Alexander, was educated by Erasmus and made Archbishop of St Andrews.

According to a Spanish ambassador who saw the King in the middle 1490s, James IV was 'as handsome in complexion and shape as a man can be'. He was tall and red-haired as Dunbar described him, and although all surviving portraits show him as clean-shaven, the Spaniard observed : 'He never cuts his hair or beard; it becomes him very well.'

In the early years of the reign, relations between Scotland and England were troubled. Henry VII may have expected an inimical attitude on the part of the regime which had overthrown his late ally James III. He encouraged a plot by Ramsay of Balmain to seize James IV and send him as a prisoner to England. The plot failed, but James retaliated by supporting the Yorkist pretender Perkin Warbeck.

Warbeck arrived in Scotland in 1495, and the following year James IV invaded England on his behalf and proclaimed him 'Richard IV'. Perhaps James felt that Edward IV's recognition of his traitorous uncle Albany as 'Alexander IV' of Scotland had left a score to be settled. The subjects of Henry VII, however, had enjoyed ten years of peace, and they had no wish to experience a renewal of the Wars of the Roses. They refused to rise for 'Richard IV', and the invasion from Scotland was a failure. Warbeck left Scotland in 1497.

Henry VII was nonetheless sufficiently impressed by James IV's powers of making trouble to revert to a peace policy. He offered James the hand of his elder daughter, Margaret, for which James had little enthusiasm, as he was planning to marry his mistress, Margaret Drummond. She would have been an acceptable choice, for Drummond ladies had been Queens of David II and

Robert III; however, she died in 1500, possibly poisoned by enemies of her family. In 1502 James agreed to treaties of marriage and perpetual peace with England.

In 1503 James, at the age of thirty, married Margaret Tudor, who was thirteen. An illumination in the *Book of Hours of James IV* shows her as a white-skinned, red-haired girl of delicate appearance; later portraits show her as a plump young woman with a marked resemblance to her brother Henry VIII. In ten years of marriage Margaret bore her husband six children, one of whom survived to become James V. The marriage was not happy, for Margaret had an ineradicable nostalgia for England and never attempted to identify herself with her adoptive country. But the political consequences were unhappier than the personal ones, for when James IV signed the peace treaty with England, he refused to repudiate the 'auld alliance' between Scotland and France. He regarded the link with France as an insurance against Scotland's becoming a satellite of England; yet only as long as England and France, traditional enemies, should remain at peace would his position be tenable.

The decade between the King's marriage and its tragic outcome was a time of peace and increasing prosperity, and of a great cultural flowering in Scotland. Since the early 1490s James IV had shown himself to be the guiding spirit of the kingdom, and he led it forward into a remarkable period of achievement.

In 1494 he was associated with Bishop Elphinstone of Aberdeen in the foundation of Aberdeen University. Two years later he was responsible for the first compulsory education act, which obliged all 'barons and freeholders that are of substance' to send their eldest sons to school to acquire 'perfect Latin', and after to one of the three universities – St Andrews, Glasgow or Aberdeen – to study 'art and jure [law]'. The purpose was to create a class of law-conscious administrators.

In 1505 the College of Surgeons was founded in Edinburgh and granted a royal charter, and in 1507 the printing-press was introduced to Scotland with the King's encouragement. Chepman and Myllar, Scotland's first printers, published the works of

Chaucer and of the Scottish Renaissance poets Robert Henrysoun, the greatest luminary of the previous reign, and William Dunbar.

Besides patronizing education and literature, James IV spent lavishly upon building. At Falkland, Stirling and Linlithgow he added to buildings which dated from the previous reign, and the Palace of Holyroodhouse was begun in preparation for his marriage.

Nor did James IV neglect military matters. He added to the already impressive train of royal artillery, and his desire to make Scotland a maritime power led him to sacrifice all the oakwoods of Fife to build the largest warship of the age, the *Great Michael*.

James IV's unrealized ambition was to unite the sovereigns of Europe in a crusade against the Turks. After the half century of Turkish expansion which had followed the fall of Constantinople in 1453, it was an ambition which showed an intelligent understanding of the international situation. Besides holding back the Turks at the limits of Eastern Europe, the crusade would have served to keep the peace among the rulers of Western Europe, a matter with which James IV was vitally concerned.

As the sixteenth century progressed, James watched with alarm the local quarrels of his fellow sovereigns leading irrevocably towards European war. In 1508 Pope Julius II, mistakenly desirous to increase the secular power of the Papacy, formed the league of Cambrai with France, to humble the power of Venice. Then, having failed to control the hostilities he had organized, Julius in 1511 formed the mis-named Holy League to expel the French from Italy again. The Papacy, Spain, Venice, England and the Holy Roman Empire were leagued against France, and James IV faced the consequence of having maintained alliances with both France and England. James used all his diplomatic influence to restore peace, but his attempts were in vain, and as France faced attack from all sides, King Louis XII desperately appealed for help from Scotland, his only ally.

The new King of England, Henry VIII, who had succeeded in 1509, had treated James IV in a high-handed and bellicose manner since the beginning of the reign. Deteriorating relations between Scotland and England decided James in favour of the 'auld alliance'. When Henry VIII invaded France in 1513, James sent him an ultimatum. Henry's furious reply that he was 'the very owner' of Scotland and that when he returned from France he would 'expulse' James from his kingdom, showed that if France were defeated, the independence of Scotland would be at stake again.

At the end of August 1513 James invaded England, to encounter an English army commanded by the Earl of Surrey. On 9 September James IV and a multitude of his subjects, prominent and obscure, met their death in the holocaust of Flodden.

If Bannockburn was Scotland's greatest victory against the English, Flodden was her greatest defeat at English hands. Like the army which had followed Robert I to Bannockburn, the army which marched to Flodden contained a cross-section of the population – Highlanders and Islesmen as well as Lowlanders – for no King since Robert I had been so successful as James IV in uniting the nation. The loyalty of the north-west, hard-won by a Gaelic-speaking King, was lost again in the minority of his son.

As the enemy of the Pope, James IV died under excommunication, and his body, which was found on the battlefield and sent to England, was denied Christian burial. Perhaps because the mortal remains of James IV were never seen in Scotland, the belief arose that he had survived Flodden. Reluctant to accept the loss of so beloved a King, the Scots wove the fantasy that he had gone on a pilgrimage to Jerusalem and would one day return. As the years passed, the legend changed and grew. James IV became to the Scots what King Arthur had become to the English, *Rex, Quondam Rexque Futurus* : the Once and Future King, who had been miraculously preserved, to return when his people's need was greatest.

James V: The Last King of Catholic Scotland

King James V was seventeen months old when the widowed Queen and the depleted nobility attended his coronation in the Chapel Royal of Stirling, on 21 September 1513.

Under the terms of James IV's will, Queen Margaret became *tutrix* or guardian of the King, a position which made her the head of state. But her authority was scarcely acceptable, for she was known to be the devoted sister of Henry VIII, whose intentions towards Scotland had been made plain at the outset of the Flodden campaign.

The surviving leaders of the nobility turned to France for help and requested the Franco-Scottish John Stuart, Duke of Albany, to assume the governorship. Albany was the son of James III's traitorous brother, by his French duchess, and he was the King's nearest kinsman (see Genealogical Table No 4). He redeemed the evil reputation associated with his name by providing an isolated example of political honesty in a period of self-seeking and intrigue.

Albany arrived in Scotland in 1515. In the meantime France and England had made peace, by a treaty in which Scotland was included. But although the threat of attempted English conquest was removed, English and French interests struggled for supremacy in Scotland throughout the minority of James V.

Between 1515 and 1524 Albany spent three periods of residence in Scotland. His policy was to preserve the independence of his young cousin's kingdom through maintaining the 'auld alliance'. To this end he negotiated in 1521 the Treaty of Rouen, whereby James V was to marry a daughter of François Ier of France.

Albany's chief opponents in Scotland were Queen Margaret, who saw herself as Henry VIII's vicereine, ruling Scotland as a satellite of England, and Margaret's second husband, Archibald Douglas, sixth Earl of Angus, whom the Queen had married in 1514, in the hope of gaining a pro-English supporter against her Francophile rivals. Angus was pro-English, but his policy was to gain power for himself, not to share it with Margaret. A power struggle between Angus and Margaret greatly assisted Albany's policy.

Albany left Scotland in 1524, and François Ier's demands upon his services in the Italian wars prevented his return. Angus gained power by a *coup d'état* at the end of 1525, and the following year the fourteen-year-old James v was declared of age and responsible for the government. His investiture with the symbols of sovereignty was a meaningless charade, for in effect he was Angus's prisoner, and remained so until 1528.

In a period of so much political unrest James v had a troubled childhood. He had lost his father in infancy, and he seldom saw his capricious mother, who obtained a divorce from Angus and married a third husband, Lord Methven. James v was poorly educated by comparison with the previous royal Jameses, but he became a good musician and an outstandingly fine performer in the lists. Angus, his stepfather, was culpable for the neglect of his education, and Angus was also blamed for arranging James's early sexual initiation and for encouraging him in every form of self-indulgence, in the hope of postponing or even preventing the young King's proper assertion of his authority.

Fortunately Angus's irresponsible policy failed, for James had a strong awareness of his kingship. In the early summer of 1528 James fled in disguise from his stepfather's custody, and within a few months Angus and his principal kinsmen were driven from Scotland. They took refuge in England and were well received by Henry viii. James, at the age of sixteen, began to rule his kingdom.

In appearance James v was universally acknowledged to be extremely handsome; he had red hair, fine aquiline features and steely-grey eyes. In character he was cold and ruthless, though he possessed a great deal of superficial charm. He had easy success with women, but in neither men nor women does he seem to have inspired loyalty or devotion.

The unfortunate consequences of James's experiences at the hands of Angus was his inflexible determination to rule his nobility with a strong hand; he never learned the value of winning supporters but relied upon harsh disciplinary measures which gradually made him feared and hated by most of his influential subjects. 'Sore-dread' and 'ill-beloved' were the contemporary adjectives.

His discipline, however, benefited the country as a whole. In 1529 and 1530 rough justice was used to restore order to the

Highlands, the Isles and the Border, where violence had grown
during the troubled years of the minority. For the most part,
quiet ensued throughout the reign, until a rebellion in the north-
west in 1539, led by a chief named Donald Gorme of Sleat who
claimed the Lordship of the Isles, led the King to undertake one
of his most ambitious projects – a circumnavigation of the north,
to make the royal power a reality in the remotest areas of the
kingdom. In 1540 he visited Orkney, rounded Cape Wrath to
land on many of the Western Isles and concluded his voyage at
Dumbarton, bringing back with him many prisoners and hostages, to ensure the future good behaviour of the Highland and
Island chiefs. After his return the Lordship of the Isles was
finally annexed to the Crown.

Though James v became unpopular with the nobility, the
commons loved him as their protector. Certainly his concern for
the welfare of his people made his popularity with them well
deserved. It gained an extra dimension through his habit of
wandering among them in the guise of a farmer, 'the Gudeman
o' Ballengeich.' Perhaps he was less successfully disguised than
he supposed, for 'The Gudeman o' Ballengeich' became almost
a synonym for 'the King'; at least disguise provided the means
of informality and enabled James to share his people's pleasures
and observe their hardships.

It is useless, however, to be the champion of the weak without
the support of at least some of the strong. Alienated from the
nobility, James v came to rely increasingly upon the clergy. Yet
this policy too was in the nature of building a house upon sand,
for by the early sixteenth century the Church in Scotland was in
a supine condition. As James v's reign progressed, Scotland
became increasingly receptive to Protestant opinions. The
Reformation was approaching, though James v, in common with
other rulers, imagined that the religion of the kingdom was the
King's decision. (Henry viii admitted the Reformation to
England; whether he could have kept it out is another matter.)

James v chose Catholicism and was handsomely rewarded for
his orthodoxy. With papal approval he was able to impose a tax
of £10,000 a year on the Scottish prelates, upon the pretext

that the money was to endow a 'College of Justice', or a body of salaried professional judges in Scotland. Most of the aptly named 'Great Tax' went not to the judges but to the King. Furthermore, five of James's illegitimate sons were made commendators, or lay-abbots, of the richest Scottish abbeys, to the increasing enrichment of the King and the increasing enfeeblement of the Church upon which the King relied.

In his foreign policy James v turned to the 'auld alliance', the obvious bulwark against the power of his anti-papal uncle, Henry viii. James visited France in the autumn of 1536, and on 1 January 1537, in accordance with the Treaty of Rouen, he married Madeleine, the daughter of François 1er. Madeleine was a delicate girl, but her determination to be Queen of Scotland and James's determination to marry a daughter of France overcame François's fears for her health. Tragically, those fears proved justified, for Madeleine died on 7 July. The following year James married a second French bride, the beautiful and intelligent Marie de Guise. She bore him two sons, both of whom died in 1541; in 1542 she gave birth to the daughter who lived to reign as Mary, Queen of Scots.

The generous dowries which James v received with his two French Queens enabled him to give visual expression to the inspiration he had derived from his visit to France. Between 1537 and 1542 James attempted to metamorphose the royal residences of Scotland into renaissance *châteaux*. Elegant buildings from his reign survive at Stirling and Falkland : the latter, in particular, has been described as 'the finest monument to the auld alliance'.

James v's years of prosperity were merely a prelude to disaster. Relations between Scotland and England began to deteriorate again in 1541. Soon a configuration of international alliances was formed in which James v was the ally of François 1er and Henry viii the ally of François's enemy the Emperor Charles v. Scotland and England were being forced into war almost as they had been in 1513. The difference was that James v was the ally of the Pope, and many of the Scottish nobility in the course of the reign had embraced Protestantism.

When war broke out between Scotland and England, James v's Protestant nobles proved unwilling to fight for an ill-beloved King against their co-religionists.

In the autumn of 1542 Henry VIII sent an army – fatefully commanded by the son of the victor of Flodden – to invade Scotland. At the same time he renewed the old claim of over-lordship. James gathered his forces and marched south to meet the enemy. But despite English provocation, the Scottish nobility refused to invade England. The army disbanded at Fala Muir, and the King returned humiliated to Edinburgh. A second force, raised by the King's clerical supporters, invaded England on the west, only to be defeated by a very much smaller English force at the battle of Solway Moss on 24 November 1542.

James V, who had been taken ill on the eve of the invasion, received news of the disaster on his sickbed at Lochmaben Castle. The shock of the event, and the belief that nothing pre-vented Henry VIII from conquering Scotland, seems to have caused a complete mental and physical breakdown in James V. Ill and despairing, he left Lochmaben on purposeless wanderings which brought him at last to Falkland. There he willed himself to die, on 14 December.

On his deathbed James v uttered his famous prophecy con-cerning the crown of Scotland: 'Adieu, farewell. It came with a lass, it will pass with a lass.' He imagined that the crown which had come to the Stewarts through Margery Bruce would be lost with the accession of his defenceless daughter Mary, who was one week old when he died.

It was not the Stewart crown which passed with a lass, but medieval Scotland, the Catholic Scotland of which James V was the last Catholic King. The whirlwind of the Reformation which swept Scotland in the reign of James v's daughter spared the Royal House but swept away the unhappy Queen herself.

Mary, Queen of Scots

The Regent for the infant Queen was James Stewart, second Earl of Arran, who was her nearest kinsman and heir presump-

Facsimile of the great seal of King Duncan I.
The great seal of King William 'the Lion'.

King David I (left) and his grandson King Malcolm IV 'the Maiden', from
the initial letter of the Charter of Kelso Abbey, 1159.

The coronation of King Alexander III, 1249, from a fifteenth-century manuscript of Fordun's *Scotichronicon*. The figure on the left is the *seannachie* who recited the King's genealogy.

John Balliol, puppet King of Scotland after Edward I of England's arbitration in the succession dispute, pays homage to Edward in 1292. Late fourteenth-century illumination.

Obverse and reverse of the great seal of King Robert I 'the Bruce'.

Contemporary illumination showing King David II shaking the hand of his captor, Edward III of England, after the battle of Neville's Cross, 1346.

Robert the 3
Begun his Rayne
1390
Maryd Anabell
Drumond
dochter of [...]robhall

King Robert III and his Queen Annabella Drummond, as represented in the late sixteenth-century *Seton Armorial*.

King James I, one of a series of portraits of the first five Jameses, painted in the sixteenth century by an unknown artist working from earlier likenesses.

IACOBVS·I·D·GRAT
REX·SCOTORVM

Contemporary drawing of King James II by Jörg von Ehingen, a German visitor to the Court of Scotland.

Jacob von gots genaden künig von Schottland

Opposite King James III at his devotions, attended by St Andrew, patron of Scotland, from the Trinity College altarpiece by Hugo van der Goes. The boy kneeling behind the King may be either his eldest son, later James IV, or one of his brothers. *Above* Contemporary drawing of King James IV by Jacques le Boucq, from the *Recueil d'Arras*.

James the fyrst
began his raig[n]
1514 He maryed
Magdelena dothe[r]
of francis ye furst
k. of france

Opposite King James v and his first Queen, Madeleine of France, from the *Seton Armorial*.

Miniature of King James v by an unknown artist, probably copied from a contemporary portrait.

Marie de Guise, second Queen of James v and mother of Mary, Queen of Scots, detail from a contemporary double portrait of James v and Marie de Guise.

Mary, Queen of Scots, portrait by an unknown artist, *c.* 1560–5.

King James VI as a chi
attributed to Rowla
Lockey.

King James VI and I
Garter robes, by Dan
Mytens, c. 1621–23.

The Lyte Jewel, enamelled gold locket set with diamonds, containing a miniature of King James VI and I, attributed to Nicholas Hilliard, *c.* 1610. The jewel was given by the King to Thomas Lyte of Lyte's Carey, Somerset, as a reward for tracing the genealogy of the Kings of Britain.

Anne of Denmark, consort of James VI and I, attributed to William Larkin. This portrait probably shows the Queen in mourning for her elder son, Prince Henry, who died in 1612.

This page:
King Charles I in three positions, painted by Van Dyck, to serve as a model for Bernini's portrait-bust of the King.

Henrietta Maria, consort of Charles I, from the studio of Van Dyck.

Opposite page:
King Charles II, after J. M. Wright.

King James VII and II, portrait by Sir Peter Lely, painted before James's accession, c. 1671.

Queen Anne, detail from portrait by Michael Dahl, *c.* 1690.
Queen Mary II, after William Wissing.

King William 'III', with a candle, detail from a portrait by Gottfried
Schalcker.

James 'VIII and III', painted at the time of the abortive expedition of 1708, by Trevasini. He is shown here wearing a white wig.

Maria Clementina Sobieska, consort of James 'VIII and III', miniature by an unknown artist.

Prince Charles Edward
Stuart, portrait by Loui
Gabriel Blanchet.

Prince Henry Bened
Stuart, Cardinal-Duke
York, portrait aft
Batoni.

tive (see Genealogical Table No 4). Arran favoured the Protestant and English interest, and in 1543 he signed with Henry VIII a treaty by which Mary was to marry Henry's son, the future Edward VI.

The Queen-Dowager Marie de Guise and her astute adviser Cardinal Beaton, who had been temporarily eclipsed after the death of James V, quickly reasserted their influence, and the treaty with England was repudiated before the end of the year. Henry retaliated with two invasions, in 1544 and 1545. The Scots wryly termed the atrocities and devastations committed in the Borders and the Lothians 'the Rough Wooing'. Cardinal Beaton was murdered with English encouragement in 1546, but when Henry VIII himself died the following year, Scotland was still as far as ever from being England's northern province. The Regent for the boy-king Edward VI invaded Scotland in 1547 and inflicted a heavy defeat upon the Scots at the battle of Pinkie. Marie de Guise and her supporters appealed for help from France, which was granted on condition that the little Queen should be sent to France for her education and married to the Dauphin François, the eldest son of King Henri II.

Mary, Queen of Scots sailed for France in 1548. At the Court of Henri II and his Queen, Catherine de' Medici, and in the household of her Guise grandmother, Mary received the education of a renaissance princess. She learned to speak and write French, Latin and Italian. French, indeed, became more familiar to her than her native Scots. Ronsard taught her the art of verse-making. The culture, and the Catholicism, of the French Court formed her mental attitudes. Adored, admired and protected, Mary spent an essentially happy childhood in France; but it may be doubted whether her sheltered upbringing prepared her for the task of ruling better than the terrors of capture and *coup d'état* had prepared the five Jameses. In 1558, at the age of sixteen, Mary married the Dauphin François, and by a secret agreement she pledged that if she should die without issue Scotland should become subject to the crown of France.

In the meantime, Marie de Guise had been striving to preserve the Catholic kingdom of Scotland as her daughter's

K. & Q.—4

inheritance. Her daughter's rights concerned her more than Scotland's independence, and if they could be preserved by the subjection of Scotland to France, Marie would have considered the sacrifice worthwhile. Marie de Guise superseded Arran as Regent of Scotland in 1554, and from that date until the Reformation the 'auld alliance' bound the two kingdoms more closely together than ever before.

In 1559 Henri II was accidentally killed at a tournament, and Queen Mary's husband became François II of France. Briefly Mary was both Queen Regnant of Scotland and Queen Consort of France. But in June 1560 Marie de Guise died, and her death was followed by that of François II at the end of the year. The eighteen-year-old Mary was politically insignificant as Queen-Dowager of France. In Scotland she would be a reigning sovereign; but her native kingdom offered a dangerous challenge.

The death of Marie de Guise had coincided with the Reformation rebellion in Scotland, in which the Earl of Arran (now also Duke of Châtelherault), the Calvinist reformer John Knox and Mary's half-brother, the Lord James Stewart, an illegitimate son of James V, all played leading parts. With timely assistance from the new Queen Elizabeth I of England, the Reformers triumphed in Scotland. When Mary, Queen of Scots, sailed from France, to arrive at Leith on 19 August 1561, as a Catholic Queen she was at least an object of suspicion to the new order.

Mary had certain assets. Her auburn hair, fine features and fair skin, her courtly accomplishments, her elegant horsemanship, her charm, *esprit* and courage, all won her the admiration of her subjects. And she had good advice and followed it wisely. Lord James Stewart, whom she created Earl of Moray, and her Secretary of State, William Maitland of Lethington, both advised her to follow a conciliatory policy in religion : to retain her Mass as her sovereign privilege and to give official recognition to the reformed religion. Mary accepted their advice, and in the early years of her reign she prospered.

Lethington's policy was to win her recognition as the successor of the 'Virgin Queen' Elizabeth I. As grand-daughter of Margaret Tudor, Mary had a strong claim to the English succession. In the eyes of Catholic Europe her claim was superior to that of Elizabeth, who, as the child of Henry VIII's second marriage to Anne Boleyn, was from the Catholic viewpoint illegitimate. Elizabeth, for obvious reasons, had no wish to recognize Mary's claim, but for some years the delicate question was debated without rancour.

Mary's difficulties began with her choice of a husband. After abortive negotiations with several European princes, Mary chose her cousin, Henry Stuart, Lord Darnley (see Genealogical Table No 4). Darnley, whom Mary married on 29 July 1565, was also a grandchild of Margaret Tudor. By her second marriage to the Earl of Angus, Queen Margaret had one child, Lady Margaret Douglas, who married Matthew Stuart, fourth Earl of Lennox. Their son, Lord Darnley, who was brought up in England, had reversionary claims to the thrones of both Scotland and England. In theory Mary, Queen of Scots, had made an intelligent choice, for the marriage of the two cousins would strengthen the claim of their descendants to the English throne.

In practice, however, the marriage was disastrous, for though Darnley was a handsome young man with some accomplishments, he was arrogant, self-indulgent and possessed of an inexhaustible talent for making enemies. He immediately alienated the Earl of Moray and many other members of the nobility. Soon he quarrelled with the Queen and accused her of infidelity with her secretary, David Riccio.

On 9 March 1566 Darnley, together with the Earl of Morton, Lords Lindsay, Ruthven and others, broke into the Queen's apartments at Holyrood and murdered Riccio, who had become something of a *bête noir* as an influential foreigner and a suspected papal agent. Mary, who was six months pregnant with the child begotten by Darnley before the Riccio scandal was even thought of, never forgave her husband for endangering her life by committing murder in her presence or for smirching her reputation.

After the birth of Mary and Darnley's son, Prince James, on 19 June 1566, Mary began to contemplate the possibility of ending her marriage to her violent and degenerate husband. In her disillusionment with Darnley she showed increasing favour to James Hepburn, Earl of Bothwell, a rugged but not altogether uncivilized man, who gave her the reassurance of loyalty, as well as attracting her by the contrast he presented with Darnley.

The Queen may have accepted that it was expedient Darnley should die if she were to be free of him without endangering the legitimacy of her son by a divorce. Darnley died on 10 February 1567, when the house in which he was sleeping, at Kirk o' Field on the outskirts of Edinburgh, was blown up by an unnecessarily massive quantity of gunpowder. He himself was found in the garden, uninjured by the blast but killed by strangulation. The extent of the Queen's foreknowledge or complicity has remained a mystery. Darnley had many enemies, including the other murderers of Riccio whom he had abandoned in an attempt to recover the Queen's good graces; but the chief suspect, then and thereafter, was the Earl of Bothwell.

Mary, Queen of Scots, sacrificed her reputation when she married Bothwell, on 15 May 1567, after he had been tried and acquitted for the murder of Darnley, and after he had divorced his wife, Lady Jean Gordon. The best explanation of Mary's apparently insensate behaviour is that she was pregnant by Bothwell, and since it was known that she had been estranged from Darnley since the murder of Riccio, the child could not have been her husband's. The fact that she miscarried of twins in July 1567 gives colour to this hypothesis.

Mary's marriage to Bothwell caused a coalescence of opposition in the name of Prince James. On 15 June Mary and Bothwell faced James's supporters on the field of Carberry Hill, near Musselburgh. The Queen was defeated by the desertion of her own troops. She was taken as a prisoner to Edinburgh and afterwards incarcerated in the island fortress of Lochleven, where she was forced to abdicate in favour of her son, on 24 July.

Mary made a dramatic escape from Lochleven on 2 May 1568. She swiftly gathered an army of supporters and met the forces of her alienated half-brother Moray at the battle of Langside, near Glasgow, on 13 May. Mary was defeated. She rode south-westwards from the battlefield and sailed across the Solway

Firth to take refuge in England. Elizabeth had shown sympathy for her during her captivity, and Mary may have hoped, even expected, that Elizabeth would assist in her restoration. She was destined to disappointment.

Her entertainment in England gradually changed from courteous detainment into close captivity. Perhaps it was in the early days of her residence in England that Mary, Ronsard's pupil, sought to win Elizabeth's sympathy with a sonnet urging that they should meet. Face to face with Elizabeth she might plead her cause effectively.

> One thought sustains my hours of solitude,
> Yet sweet and bitter grows my mood in turn;
> Doubt freezes me, and then with hope I burn,
> Till sleep and rest my aching heart elude.
> Dear Sister, see how I lack quietude :
> Desire to meet with you oppresses me;
> The torment of delay distresses me.
> Let my words end this long incertitude!
> I've seen a ship blown wildly from her course,
> In sight of port, but 'ere she came to land
> Driven again into the raging sea.
> Likewise I fear to come to grief perforce.
> Oh, do not think I fear it at your hand!
> But Fate can mar the fairest destiny.*

It was the fears and not the hopes which proved justified. Elizabeth never received her, and Mary was kept a prisoner in England for nineteen years. With some justification she plotted to obtain her release, her reinstatement in her own kingdom, even her establishment upon the English throne as the legitimist Catholic claimant. Her participation in the plot initiated by Anthony Babington to assassinate Elizabeth and crown Mary as Queen of England eventually led to her death. Elizabeth, who shrank from the execution of a sovereign, was at last compelled by the force of public and ministerial opinion to concede to Mary's death.

* Author's translation.

The Queen of Scots was executed at Fotheringay on 8 February 1587.

🌿 *James VI: The Triumph of Intellect*

James VI was crowned in the church of the Holy Rude at Stirling on 29 July 1567. His coronation by newly devised Protestant rites was the logical conclusion of the Reformation rebellion of 1560. Moray and his supporters, having exploited Queen Mary's matrimonial misadventures in a ruthless manner to secure her deposition, had obtained what they wanted in the person of her son: an infant King who could be moulded into the ideal Reformation ruler. That James VI did not turn out exactly as they had expected was not for lack of trying.

James VI was brought up in Stirling Castle, under the care of John Erskine, Earl of Mar. James was a frail child with a poor physique and a good intellect. He is believed to have suffered from rickets, and in consequence of this complaint to have lacked dignity and grace of movement; but he was not the grotesque figure which he is sometimes represented as having been. He was educated by George Buchanan, a great classical scholar but an irascible disciplinarian. A significant part of Buchanan's task was to teach James to regard his deposed mother as an enemy. Buchanan, who detested the Queen, carried it out with gusto, sometimes allowing his feelings to lead him into unjust severity towards Mary's son. While he crammed James remorselessly with Latin, Greek, history and Calvinist theology, Buchanan also tried to inculcate into his pupil *avant garde* ideas on the rights of the subject against a tyrannous king. James, who was clever and obstinate, absorbed the learning but repudiated the political theory. He took his stand upon the Divine Right of Kings, the opposing theory which stressed the subject's duty of obedience and the King's responsibility to God alone.

The lonely young King was fairly safe in the fastness of Stirling, but the country was in turmoil around him. The violent events which punctuated his minority, while his adherents fought a civil war against the remaining supporters of his mother, left him with a nervous terror of violence which lasted for the rest of his life.

Four regents ruled Scotland for James VI: the Earl of Moray, who was assassinated in 1570; the King's grandfather, the Earl of Lennox, who was killed in an affray in 1571; the Earl of Mar, who died, apparently of natural causes, in 1572; and the Earl of Morton, who successfully imposed his authority for some years. A *coup d'état* led by the Earls of Argyll and Atholl ousted Morton from the regency in 1578, but he swiftly reasserted himself and remained in power until 1580.

The King experienced the first happiness in his life through his love for his Franco-Scottish cousin Esmé Stuart d'Aubigny (see Genealogical Table No 4), who visited Scotland in 1579. Captivated by his charm, James showered him with honours culminating in the dukedom of Lennox, bestowed on him in 1581. It was Lennox and his henchman Captain James Stewart who organized Morton's downfall. Morton was accused of participation in the murder of Darnley; he admitted fore-knowledge, for which he was executed.

Lennox, as a Catholic, was an object of suspicion to the Protestant Kirk and nobility, who imagined that he had come to Scotland to work for the restoration of Queen Mary. Despite his efforts to allay suspicion by undergoing conversion, Lennox's influence was ended in 1582 by a *coup* in which the King was seized and held prisoner by William Ruthven, Earl of Gowrie, and other Protestant lords. Lennox was driven from the country and died in France the following year. For ten months James remained a grief-stricken captive. But at the age of seventeen he aspired to rule his kingdom, and in June 1583 he escaped and asserted his authority, with the assistance of Captain James Stewart, whom he created Earl of Arran.

Early in his personal rule James VI revealed the preoccupation which obsessed him increasingly as the years passed: his claim to the English succession. Like his mother, he ardently desired to be recognized as the heir of Elizabeth I. In the hope of winning recognition, he began from 1585 onwards to cultivate closer relations with England. Elizabeth, who distrusted Arran

as an adventurer, encouraged the *coup d'état* by which he fell
from power in 1585. James then formed an administration in
which most acceptable shades of political and religious opinion
were represented. With the able assistance of his Chancellor,
John Maitland of Thirlestane, he began to emerge as the
'Universal King' which he aspired to be, no longer the tool of a
dominant faction.

In 1586 a formal league was concluded with England, and
though Elizabeth steadfastly refused to recognize James as her
heir, she began to pay him a pension of £4,000 a year, and
allowed him to understand that his prospects were improving.
Such was the delicate situation between James VI and Elizabeth
when the complicity of the captive Queen of Scots in the
Babington conspiracy was revealed.

James's attitude to his mother was ambivalent. He had tried
to reject Buchanan's view of her as an adulteress and a mur-
deress; yet he had never known her and he could not love her. As
long as she lived, he could not feel secure, either as King of Scots
or as prospective heir of England. He sent Elizabeth a strong
protest against her execution; but he took no other action. Many
years later he tried to quieten his uneasy conscience by giving
her a magnificent tomb in Westminster Abbey.

James's aspiration to the English throne likewise dictated his
attitude to the Spanish Armada of 1588. Friendly neutrality was
his official policy towards England; but he knew that his
Catholic nobles, led by the Earl of Huntly, for whom he had
affection, were in communication with Philip II of Spain. In the
event of a Spanish victory, he hoped that his favour to Huntly
might give him a chance of survival. The crisis was averted by
the defeat of the Armada, and relations with England were
unimpaired.

In 1589 James VI was able to leave Scotland for several
months, when he sailed to Oslo to marry Anne of Denmark, the
bride of his choice, after his marriage had been under discussion
for several years. When James and his Queen returned to
Scotland on May Day 1590, Anne's golden Scandinavian looks
aroused great admiration. It was unfortunate that her intellect

was by far inferior to her husband's. James had been taught by George Buchanan, who was a dour misogynist, to hold feminine intelligence in contempt, and Queen Anne's delight in clothes, jewels and dancing did nothing to cause her husband to change his opinion. In later years her taste matured, and as Queen of England she became the valued patroness of Inigo Jones. Though she may have appreciated the brilliant spectacle of the Court masques which he created for her more than his genius as an architect, it should not be forgotten that Queen's House at Greenwich was begun for Anne of Denmark.

Queen Anne bore James seven children, of whom three survived infancy: Prince Henry, who died in 1612, Princess Elizabeth (the future Queen of Bohemia and ancestress of the House of Hanover) and Prince Charles (the future Charles I).

During the later years of James VI's reign in Scotland, his principal preoccupations were the relations between Kirk and State, the imposing of law and order and the all-important question of the English succession.

Under the leadership of Andrew Melville, a more uncompromising disciple of Calvin than John Knox, the Kirk took its cue from Calvin's Geneva and claimed to be a theocratic organization empowered to direct secular rulers. James's struggle to subject the Kirk to the control of bishops as agents of royal authority had begun as early as 1585, and it continued throughout the reign. Andrew Melville and James VI were worthily matched opponents. When Melville declared that the King was 'God's sillie vassal' (i.e., God's simple servant) and James countered with his famous dictum 'No Bishop, no King', both men crystallized their views for all time. Ultimately the King was victorious, and his bishops became Crown servants who assisted in the task of imposing law and order in the remote parts of the kingdom; but the high point of James's achievements at the expense of the Kirk was reached after his accession to the English throne.

The problem of reimposing the rule of law after the upheaval of the Reformation period and James's disordered minority at first appeared insuperable. Certain dramatic incidents illustrate the King's difficulties: for example, Huntly's murder of 'the Bonny Earl of Moray', on 7 February 1592. James was known to favour the Catholic Huntly, and he suffered much opprobrium because Moray was a Protestant, and popular. He suffered a more sustained series of trials in the attempted *coups d'état* of his unbalanced cousin Francis Stewart, Earl of Bothwell, who was a nephew of Mary's Bothwell and an illegitimate grandson of James v. Bothwell may have aspired to the throne, but his attempts to make use concurrently of the alliance of the Kirk, the friendship of Huntly and the black magic rituals of the 'North Berwick Witches' ultimately led to his downfall. He was forced to leave Scotland in 1595, and died in exile. The last attempt to subvert James vi's government was the mysterious 'Gowrie Plot' of 1600, which may have involved an unsuccessful attempt upon the King's life.

These dramas, however, were merely interruptions of the King's sustained and in the main successful effort to improve the administration of his kingdom and the daily lives of his subjects. The rule of law slowly superseded that of tooth and claw, until some years after James became King of England he was able to write: 'This I may say for Scotland, and may truly vaunt it: here I sit and govern it with my pen. I write and it is done, and by a Clerk of the Council I govern Scotland now, which others could not do by the sword.' This boast both underestimated the achievements of his ancestors and overestimated his own, but there was a measure of truth in it.

Elizabeth i of England died in 1603. James vi had been in correspondence with her chief minister, Robert Cecil, for the past two years, and the way for his accession had been made smooth. Whether or not Elizabeth acknowledged James as her heir on her deathbed is a matter of some doubt, but Cecil had seen to it that whether she did so or not would be of little moment. James vi of Scotland was proclaimed James i of England without incident. England, the 'auld enemy', had at the last become subject to a King of Scots, instead of Scotland to a King of England, as had so often seemed more likely.

5

THE HOUSE OF STUART

1603-1707

🦌 The First King of Great Britain

From the earliest likeness of a small red-haired, bleak-faced boy with a hawk on his wrist, to the last picture of a disillusioned old King sitting slumped in his chair with his hands dangling inertly over the chair-arms, all the portraits of James vi and i are recognizably portraits of the same person. Yet accounts of the reign of James vi of Scotland and of James i of England read like accounts of the reigns of two different Kings.

In Scotland the reign of James vi had been a success story. At the time of his accession, the Crown had been impoverished, the kingdom in disorder, and warfare between the old order and the new, both actual and polemical, had been carried over into his reign. With no resources except those of his own intellect, he had triumphed over a situation which had destroyed his mother. His slight advantage, that he had been brought up in the religion of the winning side, would not alone have been enough to decide the issue in his favour. His achievement was his own.

In England the reign of James i was not a success story : it was a story of initial promise followed by failure. The new King came south with a great and deserved reputation for learning, to which were added the laurels of authorship. He had published two volumes of verse : *Essayes of a Prentise in the Divine Art of Poesie* and *His Majestie's Poetical Exercises at Vacant Houres* (his talent as a poet was slight, but a few of his verses are illumined by a genuine spark); he had written *Daemonologie*, warning his subjects of the snares of satanism and witchcraft; and he had contributed to political theory with *The Trew Law of Free Monarchies* and *Basilikon Doron*.

He arrived in England with a dual reputation, that of an intellectual and successful King and that of a foreigner. His foreignness was accentuated by his coming to England accompanied by a horde of Scots ambitious for advancement. He favoured his Scottish kinsmen and courtiers, and identified himself with them,

continuing to talk Scots broadly enough for his English subjects
to find difficulty in understanding him.

James found the Church of England very much to his liking.
The unique relationship between the English sovereign and the
established Church, and the fact that the Church was docile,
ceremonious and governed by bishops, won the new King's
approval. His relations with other institutions were not com-
mensurately happy. His troubles with the English Parliament,
though they lie outside the scope of this book, contributed to the
decline of his reputation during his years in England and created
a difficult legacy for his successor.

His declining reputation, however, did not result only from
constitutional difficulties; as the years passed, King James
deteriorated in health, appearance and intellectual capacity.

Symptomatic of his general deterioration was his choice of
favourites. His homosexual tendencies, first revealed by his
early love for Esmé Stuart, had not during his reign in Scotland
affected his judgment of men or his choice of Crown servants.
His reign in England witnessed the depressing sight of an intelligent King enslaved by two brainless young men successively
– Somerset and Buckingham – of whom the latter was the worse,
supremely powerful and supremely incompetent. However, the
King's deterioration was slow, and the early years of his reign in
England were not discreditable.

Ideally James would have favoured a complete union between
Scotland and England. From the Scottish viewpoint, if a union
were desirable at all, the accession of a Scottish king to the
English throne created the most favourable circumstances in
which it could take place. In 1607 the Scottish Parliament passed
an Act of Union; the English Parliament, full of anti-Scottish
prejudice, refused to do so. The best concession which the King
could win was that subjects born after the Union of Crowns
– 'post-nati' – should have dual nationality.

Despite his disappointment over the failure of the Union,
James did his best to propagate a sense of unity between his
kingdoms. It was he who referred to the four realms of Scotland,
England, Wales and Ireland as 'Great Britain'.

When King James left Scotland in 1603, he promised to return every three years, a promise which he did not keep. It would have been well if he had kept it, for his absentee kingship created an unhappy precedent which was followed by his successors. James himself, with his long experience of ruling Scotland, was able to draw upon an intimate knowledge of his original kingdom to enable him to govern it efficiently from a distance. His successors, who did not possess the same advantage, became increasingly uncomprehending of Scotland's problems.

James VI and I, in accordance with the boast already quoted, governed Scotland with his pen, writing his instructions to the Scottish Privy Council and to the parliamentary committee known as the 'Lords of the Articles', through which he controlled the Scottish Parliament.

Yet it was inevitable that, as the years passed, his understanding of public opinion in Scotland would grow less exact. This was illustrated in particular by the course of his relations with the Kirk. His religious policy, before and after the Union of Crowns, was completely consistent: gradually he increased the number and the powers of the Scottish bishops, and he removed the most strenuous opponent of episcopacy when he summoned Andrew Melville to London in 1606 and imprisoned him for three years in the Tower of London. Wisely, James did not make a martyr of Melville, who was exiled after his release; wisely, too, he did not interfere with the worship and organization of the Kirk at the parochial level. His power over the Kirk was exerted through his manipulation of the General Assembly – the Kirk's supreme council, which was a kind of shadow Parliament, containing representatives of the three estates. It appeared that the King had metamorphosed the Kirk to the extent that he desired without arousing much antagonism.

The change came in 1617 when James paid his only return visit to Scotland. Fourteen years' happy experience of the Church of England had convinced him of its superiority, and he decided that the Kirk must be brought to resemble it more closely. Accordingly he endeavoured to force upon the Kirk the famous 'Five Articles' which decreed that Holy Communion should be received kneeling; that the Kirk should celebrate the festivals of the Christian year; that Confirmation should be performed by bishops and not by ministers; and that private Baptism and Communion should be permitted in cases of grave sickness. These apparently moderate requirements seemed, in the eyes of the Kirk, to suggest a 'popish' attitude to sacraments and festivals. They were met with vehement opposition.

King James insisted that the General Assembly which met at Perth in 1618 should adopt the Five Articles, but subsequently he did not enquire too closely into the extent to which the Five Articles were imposed in practice. To the end he did not lose some sense of how far he could and could not go.

His policy of strengthening the rule of law in Scotland was likewise consistently pursued after the Union of Crowns. The problem of Border warfare died almost of its own accord after 1603; if the Borders did not, as James had desired, become the 'Middle Shires' of a united kingdom, at least they ceased to be a bloodily debated frontier. The Highlands and Isles presented the greater problem, but James's determination to impose peace and good order was increasingly fulfilled throughout the reign. Firm to the point of ruthlessness in dealing with trouble-makers, he even executed his cousin Patrick Stewart, Earl of Orkney, the notorious 'Earl Pate', who was hanged in Edinburgh in 1615.

James vi and i died on 27 March 1625. He was not quite fifty-nine, but premature senility had robbed him of both authority and dignity. His self-indulgent habits, and his total surrender to the influence of Buckingham in his later years, had largely cost him the respect of his English subjects. In Scotland his reputation was better, for his decline had not been witnessed, and the benefits of his rule were everywhere experienced. As the tumultuous seventeenth century progressed, his reputation if anything increased; if his reign had not been a golden age, at least it had been a period of growing prosperity and peace. He was, without insincerity, referred to as 'Blessed King James'.

🏵 *Charles I*

Prince Charles, the second son of King James and Anne of Denmark, was born in the Palace of Dunfermline on 19 November 1600. Charles was a slow developer, delicate in health and troubled by a speech defect. During his childhood he was overshadowed by his brilliant elder brother, Prince Henry. After Henry's death in 1612, Charles responded to the challenge of his inheritance. He overcame his early disabilities, he became a fine horseman and during the Civil War he displayed outstanding physical courage. Though he was small in stature, his dignity and elegance made him an impressive figure. His long, dark auburn hair and his handsome melancholy face have been made familiar by the many portraits painted by Van Dyck. The best known of all, which shows three views of the King, was painted for the sculptor Bernini from whom Charles commissioned a white marble bust. When Bernini received the picture, he said 'Never have I beheld a countenance more unfortunate' – an observation which was remembered when the tragic conclusion of Charles's reign made it seem to have been prophetic.

In character, though he was capable of deep feeling, Charles was withdrawn and fastidious. He was closest to his mother, who died in 1619. He loved his father, though he was critical of the loose morals, the conmingled luxury and squalor and the general disorder of the Jacobean Court. Everything changed when he became King in 1625. In the words of a contemporary memoirist : 'King Charles was temperate, chaste and serious, so that the fools and bawds, the mimics and catamites of the former Court, grew out of fashion. . . .'

In 1626 Charles I married Henrietta Maria, the daughter of Henri IV of France and Marie de' Medici. Henrietta, as her biographer neatly put it, is best described by four untranslatable French words, '*chic, petite, difficile* and *dévote*'. Van Dyck's portraits of Henrietta have made her appearance almost as familiar as that of Charles himself. They suggest that the tiny, dark-haired Queen had an irresistible charm and grace which did not depend upon conventional beauty. The marriage was supremely happy, but Henrietta's tactlessly ardent Catholicism proved an increasing liability to her husband's cause.

Charles I's English subjects did not forget that he had been born in Scotland – they were constantly reminded by his Scots accent. To that extent he was a foreigner. To the Scots, however, he was even more a foreigner. He had been brought up in England and his knowledge of Scotland derived only from the expatriate Scottish lords at the English Court. In 1625 Scotland acquired a native but absentee King, whose connection with his kingdom was extremely attenuated.

Charles I conceived it his duty to complete the task begun by his father of anglicanizing the Scottish Kirk. What James VI and I had seen in terms of political advantage and personal preference, Charles I saw in terms of religious duty. To Charles Presbyterianism was merely a deplorable sub-species of Protestantism, which ought to be brought into line, forcibly if necessary, with Anglicanism.

As a first step towards making proper provision for the Church in Scotland which he envisaged, Charles made an Act of Revocation in 1625. It had been the custom of Scottish kings to revoke all grants made during their minorities when they reached the age of twenty-five; a reasonable measure, since such grants might have been made under duress. Charles I's Act, however, was extraordinarily sweeping, for it revoked all grants of Church lands made since the Reformation. While Charles thus alienated very many of the Scottish nobility, the 'Lords of Erection', whose titles derived from former Church lands, he did not gain the support of the Kirk, for his anglicanizing policy was deeply suspect.

In 1633 Charles paid his first visit to Scotland since he had left thirty years before. He was crowned in St Giles with full Anglican ritual. Edinburgh was made a bishopric, and St Giles became its cathedral. Far from impressing the Scots with the excellence of the 'beauty of holiness' which the King loved, his coronation aroused in the Kirk and its adherents a renewed dread of 'popery'.

In such unpropitious circumstances Charles I and his Archbishop of Canterbury, William Laud, proposed to remake the Scottish liturgy. From their viewpoint it was a signal gesture of adaptability to acknowledge that the Kirk required a different liturgy from the Church of England. The Revised Prayer Book has been greatly praised for its dignity and beauty of language, but it represented the imposition of alien usages, and as such it was unacceptable. Its inauguration, on 23 July 1637, in St Giles, was the occasion of a riot. Charles, who did not witness it, was unmoved : he ordered the use of the Revised Prayer Book to be enforced throughout the kingdom.

He had committed an error; force invited resistance. In the autumn of 1637 a committee known as 'the Tables' was formed to resist the King's anglicanizing policy. The Earls of Rothes, Montrose and Argyll, and numerous leading ministers and lawyers, joined in objecting to King Charles's innovations. Charles I, far more out of touch with Scottish opinion than his father had ever been, resolutely ignored petitions against the new liturgy.

King Charles's refusal to read the signs of the times led to the signing of the National Covenant in 1638. Initially signed in Greyfriars' Churchyard in Edinburgh, by nobility, clergy and burgesses, on 28 February, a day described by one of its more perfervid signatories as 'the great marriage day of this nation with God', the Covenant was eventually signed through the length and breadth of the kingdom. The Covenant was not a hysterical document. It condemned specifically Catholic practices, asserted a desire for a Presbyterian polity, rejected Anglican innovations and pledged loyalty to the Crown.

A General Assembly of the Kirk met in Glasgow in 1638. The King sent the Duke of Hamilton as his Commissioner. Hamilton, recognizing the intransigent mood of the Assembly, walked out, and the Assembly deposed and excommunicated the Scottish bishops and repudiated the Revised Prayer Book. Henceforward the King could assert his wishes only by force.

The next two years witnessed the so-called 'Bishops' Wars'. The first involved no fighting and ended with the inconclusive

Pacification of Berwick, by which it was agreed that disputes between the King and the Covenanters should be referred to a new General Assembly and Scottish Parliament. Both these bodies refused to compromise, and the second Bishops' War followed. The Scottish army was commanded by Alexander Leslie and the Earl of Montrose. Leslie was a distinguished soldier with a great reputation gained in the Thirty Years' War, and James Graham, Earl of Montrose, was a military genius of the first order. Charles I's raw recruits were easily defeated.

By now Charles I was involved in much more than a religious dispute with the Scots. His government could not afford warfare without recourse to Parliament. The English Parliament had not met since 1629, and it had a long list of grievances against him and against his great minister the Earl of Strafford and Archbishop Laud. The Long Parliament, which met in 1640, impeached both Strafford and Laud. Strafford was executed in 1641 and Laud sent to the Tower.* The King faced the threat of Civil War.

In this extremity Charles I decided to sink his differences with the Covenanters and seek help in Scotland. He visited Edinburgh in the autumn of 1641, accepted the decisions of the General Assembly of 1638 to abolish episcopacy and reject the Revised Prayer Book, granted the Scottish Parliament the right (which it had already arrogated) of challenging the actions of his ministers and endeavoured to buy support by creating Leslie Earl of Leven and raising Argyll to the title of Marquess.

Civil war broke out in England in 1642. Charles's efforts to win help in Scotland had been transparently opportunist and his concessions too late to win goodwill. The Scots did not come to his assistance. Nonetheless, the Royalists were victorious in the early stages of the war. The Parliamentarians in their turn solicited the aid of the Scots.

The result was the Solemn League and Covenant of 1643. In return for a promise of £30,000 a month, the army of the Scottish Covenanters agreed to make war against the King, upon condition that Presbyterianism should be accepted in

* He was executed in 1645.

England and Ireland as well as Scotland. Charles reaped the consequences of his anglicizing policy when the Covenanters entered the Civil War for religious reasons; furthermore, much as they had objected to Charles's attempts to anglicize Scotland, they saw their own religious duty in exactly the same terms when they sought to presbyterianize England.

The Scots played a decisive part in the King's defeat at Marston Moor in 1644; but simultaneously the King's cause in Scotland gained new life, for Montrose resolved to fight for him. Montrose, whom the King gratefully created Marquess, had many bitter differences with Argyll, besides which he had not forgotten that the Covenant contained a pledge of loyalty to the Crown. The story of his brilliant year of victories against Argyll and the extremist Covenanters, especially the Highland campaign of the winter of 1644–5, has the quality of legend. But he was defeated at last at the battle of Philiphaugh in September 1645. In the meantime Charles had lost the battle of Naseby, the decisive defeat of the Royalists in England.

Montrose had not lost hope, but Charles knew that he had come to the end of his resources. In 1646 he surrendered to the Scottish army in England at Newark. He was obliged to promise that Montrose would disband his forces and leave Britain, and Montrose had no choice but to obey.

The King's situation was not quite hopeless, had he been able to see it. The reorganizing of the Parliamentarian army by Oliver Cromwell, and his great victory at Naseby, enabled the English Parliament to default upon the Solemn League and Covenant. When Charles surrendered to the Scots, they were deeply dissatisfied: they had not received their £30,000 a month, and England and Ireland were no nearer to becoming Presbyterian. If Charles could have promised what Parliament had failed to perform, the army of the Covenanters would, at this late stage, have fought for him.

Charles refused to compromise, so the Scots, to whom he had become an embarrassment, handed him over to the English and returned to Scotland having received £400,000 arrears of pay. It appeared that they had done nothing less than sell their King

Charles was confined in the Isle of Wight, and the more moderate Covenanters, shocked by the transaction at Newark, sent secret emissaries to him, to try to reach a new agreement. This time Charles was less intransigent. He can scarcely be blamed for recognizing his last chance. He agreed with the Earl of Lauderdale and the other emissaries to introduce Presbyterianism to England for a trial period of three years. This agreement was known as the 'Engagement', and the 'Engagers' hastened back to Scotland to initiate a new war on the King's behalf.

In 1648 a Scottish army led by the Duke of Hamilton invaded England, to be defeated at Preston by Oliver Cromwell. The failure of the Engagement sealed the King's fate. Charles faced trial before a tribunal which could not claim to be legally constituted. On 30 January 1649 he was executed outside the Banqueting House in Whitehall.

The news of his death was received with horror in Scotland. To fight against the King was permissible; to execute him after a travesty of justice was impermissible. The shock of the event was illustrated by the fact that when Montrose received the news, he fainted. Montrose wrote Charles's epitaph:

> Great, good and just, could I but rate
> My grief to thy too rigid fate!
> I'd weep the world in such a strain
> As it should deluge once again:
> But since thy loud-tongued blood demands supplies
> More from Briareus' hands than Argus' eyes,*
> I'll tune thy elegies to trumpet-sounds,
> And write thy epitaph in blood and wounds.

In this verse Montrose credited Charles with qualities which he had been deficient in displaying. But Charles had nonetheless possessed some impressive qualities, of which his personal virtue and the genuineness of his convictions were not the least. He came of a family which had a talent for dying well, and his

* Briareus and Argus were monsters in classical mythology: Briareus had a hundred hands and Argus a hundred eyes.

absolute courage at his execution still has the power to move all who read of it.

His 'loud-tongued blood' swiftly roused the Scots to take arms on behalf of his eldest son.

🦡 *Charles II*

Charles II was the first Stuart King to be born outside Scotland. He was born in London, in St James's Palace, on 24 May 1630. Charles was a swarthy baby, of whom his mother, Queen Henrietta Maria, half-jestingly declared that he was so dark she was ashamed of him. He grew up to have a charm which transcended unaesthetic swarthiness.

Charles was twelve at the outbreak of the Civil War. When the Royalists faced defeat, Charles obeyed his father's command to leave the country: in 1646 he sought refuge first in Jersey and then in France.

Upon receiving news of his father's trial, the exiled Prince wrote his signature at the foot of a blank sheet of paper and sent it to the English Parliament, signifying his agreement to whatever conditions might be imposed as the price of Charles I's life. That act of love and generosity expressed all that was best in his nature, and some of it died when his gesture was ignored and his father executed. Charles II was cruelly made aware that inflexible principles had to be paid for, and he did not intend to pay the same price as his father. Thenceforward opportunism played a large part in his actions.

Accordingly, he accepted the services of both Montrose and Argyll, knowing that they were enemies yet determined to use both of them to further his cause. Argyll, though he had fought against the late King, had been outraged by the manner of his death. He had Charles II proclaimed King in Edinburgh. Montrose invaded northern Scotland on Charles II's behalf, but he failed to repeat his earlier achievements. He was defeated in Carbisdale and betrayed into the hands of his enemies. Argyll had many old scores to settle, and he was not prepared to forget them in the interests of the new King. He it was who ensured

that Montrose was brought to Edinburgh, tried for treason and
hanged, in May 1649. Montrose was transparently the victim of
injustice and personal enmity, and he died as impressively as
Charles I had done.

Charles II was forced into reliance upon Argyll, concerning
whose character he can have had few illusions. In 1650 the
twenty-year-old Charles arrived in Scotland, powerless to resist
whatever demands the Covenanters might choose to make upon
him. He acquiesced in signing both Covenants, committing himself and his kingdoms to a form of religion with which he had no
more sympathy than his father. A satire published in London
made mock of Charles's situation :

> Lo, here the chicken of the eagle lies,
> Like to be made a Scottish sacrifice.
> But, wants he kingcraft to create a plot
> To undermine the sycophanting Scot?
> No, he'll a Presbyterian brother be
> And vow to ratify their hierarchy. . . .

Cromwell invaded Scotland in 1650, but his victory at Dunbar
did not prevent Charles's coronation. On New Year's Day 1651
Charles was crowned at Scone, and Argyll himself set the Crown
upon the King's head. This irregular coronation had a fateful
significance : Charles II was the last King to be crowned at
Scone, and the last to be crowned with the ancient Scottish
crown.

With a victorious enemy already in Scotland, Charles boldly
invaded England, hoping to win support for his cause as he
marched south. Cromwell followed him, and on 3 September
1651 he defeated Charles at Worcester. Charles was a closely
hunted fugitive, and it was only after many desperate adventures
that he gained the safety of France. His second exile lasted for
nine years.

Cromwell imposed a Treaty of Union upon Scotland and
England and set up in Scotland an efficient military government
which had to be maintained by high taxation and was extremely
unpopular. The standard of law and order established was im-

pressive, but the means were too much detested for the result to be appreciated. The Restoration of 1660, which restored both the King and Scotland's status as a separate kingdom, was greeted with general rejoicing.

Charles II returned to England in May, a week short of his thirtieth birthday. It is pleasant to relate that Henrietta Maria had survived to witness her son's triumph; she died in 1669.

The years of exile had increased the opportunism of Charles's character. His chief ambition was never to 'go on his travels' again. In this modest though by no means certain aim he was successful. Witty, pliant and unprincipled, he endeared himself to his English subjects by his charm, his common touch and even his human failings. The popular image of a 'Merry Monarch' with a multitude of mistresses was, however, a simplified image of a very complex character. The Scots experienced a much less benign side of it. The King himself they never saw, for he did not visit Scotland during the twenty-five remaining years of his life.

Charles II's attitude to Scotland had probably been poisoned by his experiences as a 'Covenanted King'. He had no intention of abiding by the Covenants, which he had signed under duress; indeed, he expressed the opinion that 'Presbytery was not a religion for gentlemen'.

In both kingdoms Charles was sparing in acts of vengeance. The executions of surviving regicides in England were carried out as a sop to public opinion, against the King's preference for letting bygones be bygones. In Scotland Charles permitted himself the pleasure of the execution of Argyll, who, having fought against Charles I, executed Montrose and crowned Charles II, had gone on to make his peace with Cromwell. Argyll chose to ignore the last stage of his career when he said before his death, with astounding confidence in Divine clemency, 'I set the Crown on the King's head, he hastens me now to a better crown than his.'

Charles II imitated his grandfather in governing Scotland with his pen. The chief agent of his authority was John Maitland, Earl and later Duke of Lauderdale – the erstwhile Engager –

through whom Charles sent his instructions to the Scottish Privy
Council. The Scottish Parliament was controlled as it had been
under James VI and I, by the 'Lords of the Articles'.

The Parliament of 1661 rescinded all the legislation passed
since 1633. This had the effect of restoring episcopacy and also
of reviving the pre-Covenant system of patronage, under which
ministers of the Kirk were appointed by the local laird and not
by their congregation. Unwisely, a new enactment required all
ministers appointed since 1649 to resign their livings and seek
re-appointment by their legal patrons. The consciences of a sub-
stantial minority could not be reconciled to this measure. A third
of the total number of ministers, approximately three hundred,
refused to comply and preferred to be deprived of their manses
and their livings. These resolute men, determined to uphold
both the spirit and the letter of the Covenant, enjoyed the support of their flocks, who eagerly attended the 'Conventicles' or
illegal services which began to be held secretly in farm buildings
and in lonely places out of doors.

Charles's government reacted with severity. Conventicles
were dispersed by armed force, and heavy fines imposed on those
who attended them. Repression served merely to intensify the
Covenanters' ardour. The fiercest resistance to government
policy came from Ayrshire, Lanarkshire, Dumfriesshire and
Galloway. In 1666 the Covenanters of the south-west rose in
rebellion and marched towards Edinburgh, where they were
routed at Rullion Green on the outskirts of the city. The
executions of rebel leaders which took place in Edinburgh,
Glasgow and Ayr were intended to deter sympathizers from
resorting to arms, but they were ill-judged, for they provided
the Covenanters' cause with its first group of martyrs.

In 1669 Charles sent Lauderdale to Scotland as his commissioner, to try the effect of appeasement. Lauderdale's Declarations of Indulgence, which offered the expelled ministers a chance
to resume their livings on compromise terms, failed of their
purpose. The concessions, which were both too little and too
late, were rejected by the majoriy, and persecution was resumed.

In the later years of Charles II's reign, an unhappy situation deteriorated even further. Archbishop Sharp of St Andrews was murdered by a group of Covenanters in 1679, and against all likelihood, a government force commanded by John Graham of Claverhouse, a kinsman of Montrose, was defeated by Covenanters in a skirmish at Drumclog. Charles sent his illegitimate son the Duke of Monmouth to restore order, and Monmouth inflicted a heavy defeat upon the Covenanters at Bothwell Bridge. Severe reprisals followed. Twelve hundred prisoners endured outdoor confinement in Greyfriars Churchyard in Edinburgh. About two thirds of them secured release by taking an oath of submission. The remainder, inspired doubtless by suffering in the very place where the Covenant had been signed, accepted death from exposure, execution and transportation to slavery in the West Indies, for the sake of their convictions.

The sufferings of the relatively small number of Covenanters from a limited area of Scotland earned for the last years of Charles II's reign the bitter name of 'the Killing Time'. The influence of this unhappy episode was out of all proportion to its small scope and duration. Charles II did not live to see the conclusion; he died in February 1685. During his reign Scotland had suffered increasingly from the disadvantage of an absentee monarchy, and Charles had shown himself increasingly out of touch with Scottish aspirations and problems. The unhappy history of his relations with the Covenanters is the more tragic, and the more discreditable, since in other contexts he showed himself to be a basically tolerant man.

Charles II married a Portuguese princess, Catherine of Braganza. The marriage was childless. Queen Catherine endured Charles's perpetual infidelity with exemplary dignity; she earned his respect, though she never won his love. In the absence of legitimate issue, Charles II was succeeded by his younger brother, James, Duke of York.

❦ *James VII and II*

James, who was three years younger than Charles, was born on 14 October 1633. In character he resembled his father very much more than his brother. His principles were inflexible, he possessed both integrity and courage and he was devoid of humour. He was serious-minded without being intellectual, and stupid in many ways without being altogether a fool. James shared his brother's appetite for women, but whereas Charles did not allow the pleasures of the flesh to trouble his conscience, James was oppressed by a sense of guilt. James differed from his brother in appearance as much as in character. He was fair-haired and grey-eyed, and though his features were not unlike his brother's, his somewhat immobile countenance contrasted strongly with Charles's lively and expressive face.

In the year of the Restoration James married Anne Hyde, the daughter of Edward Hyde, Earl of Clarendon, the great historian of the Civil War and Charles ii's Lord Chancellor. Clarendon's origins were middle-class, and the marriage was considered a *mésalliance*. Anne, however, triumphed over the prejudice against her and gained acceptance by the royal family. She was an intelligent and strong-minded woman whose influence upon the future extended far beyond her death in 1671.

Anne Hyde died fourteen years before her husband became King, but she bore him two daughters, Mary and Anne, both of whom were successively Queens of Great Britain. Mary and Anne were brought up as Anglicans, but their mother's conversion to Catholicism strongly influenced James, who followed her example with fanatical enthusiasm.

In 1673 James married a second time. His bride was a beautiful fourteen-year-old Italian, Mary of Modena. James had been determined to find a Catholic wife, and Mary's influence upon her husband's religious attitudes need not be over-estimated; they were already inflexibly formed.

Charles ii, secretly pro-Catholic for most of his life, was received into the Roman Church on his deathbed. James, openly a practising Catholic since 1671, succeeded on 6 February 1685, an object of suspicion as a Catholic sovereign in both Scotland and England. It is seldom remarked that only two kings of the direct Stewart-Stuart line lived and died Protestant: James vi and i and Charles i.

James vii and ii was not a complete stranger to the Scots when he became King. In 1679 he had succeeded the Duke of Lauderdale as Charles ii's commissioner in Scotland, and he had spent two periods of residence there: the winter of 1679, and a longer period from October 1680 to March 1682.

Lauderdale wrote perceptively of James: 'This good prince . . . is as very a papist as the Pope himself, which will be his ruin . . . if he had the empire of the whole world, he would venture the loss of it, for his ambition is to shine in a red letter after he is dead.'* James, who was not altogether devoid of self-knowledge even if he was devoid of political sense, admitted something similar, writing of himself in the third person:

> . . . If he had agreed to live quietly and treat his religion as a private matter . . . he could have been one of the most powerful Kings ever to reign in England . . . but, having been called by Almighty God to rule these kingdoms, he would think of nothing but the propagation of the Catholic religion . . . for which he has been and always would be willing to sacrifice everything, regardless of any mere temporal consideration.

These words provide the essential explanation of the brevity of his reign.

In Scotland, by the time James vii succeeded, the political power of the Covenanters had been broken, though widespread preference for Presbyterianism remained. Initially the King enjoyed the support of the victorious episcopal Church, which recognized its dependence on the monarchy. If James vii had been content to regard his religion as a matter of personal conviction, it is a reasonable supposition that a *modus vivendi* such as had existed during the later years of James vi would have been attained, and that the bitterness which had resulted from the Carolean persecution of the Covenanters would gradually have been forgotten. However, in Scotland as in England, James brought about his own downfall by his determination to propagate Catholicism.

* The names of major saints were printed in red in the Roman Missal; hence the saying 'A Red-Letter Day'.

James's policy in Scotland was to establish a Catholic ascendancy through the conversion of men of influence, and to secure toleration for his Catholic subjects – of whom, according to a Roman envoy in 1677, there were only two thousand between the Solway and the Moray Firth, though solidly Catholic areas survived in the Western Highlands. However, of the King's few converts most were inspired by ambition rather than convictions, and the Parliament of 1686 refused politely but firmly to grant toleration to the Catholics. James had no choice but to use the royal prerogative to carry out a policy so manifestly unpopular.

In August 1686 James granted freedom of worship to Catholics in private houses. In February 1687 he extended toleration to both Catholics and Quakers, and in June 1687, in an attempt to counteract the unpopularity of his previous measures, James granted toleration to Presbyterians.

Contrary to the King's expectations and intentions, this proclamation failed to reduce anti-Catholic feeling; rather, it raised alarm among many of the King's erstwhile supporters. The episcopal Church, which had hitherto relied upon its alliance with the Crown, saw in toleration for the Presbyterians a withdrawal of royal support. The Presbyterians, however, took courage: many, who had conformed by attending episcopalian parish churches, left them again to attend their own services, now legally permitted within doors; others, who had chosen to leave the country rather than conform, returned from Holland where they had found refuge.

Their chosen place of exile was significant. James's elder daughter Mary was married to the Dutch Prince William of Orange, who was himself the grandson of Charles I (see Genealogical Table No 5). William, a Protestant and a Stuart by descent and marriage, was an acceptable alternative for those who found a Catholic monarchy unendurable. Paradoxically, the birth of a son to Mary of Modena on 10 June 1688 sealed the fate of James VII and II. A Catholic king without an heir might have been endured as a temporary anomaly; the prospect of a Catholic dynasty was not to be contemplated.

The 'Glorious Revolution' of 1688 was the work of the English opponents of James II's Catholicizing policy; but anti-Catholic feeling made Scotland willing to participate in the overthrow of James VII. William of Orange landed at Torbay on 5 November 1688, and the following month James fled to France.

An Edinburgh mob expressed its anti-popish emotions by chasing out the Jesuits who kept a free school at Holyrood and by sacking the Catholic Chapel Royal which had been set up in the nave of Holyrood Abbey. In a passionate repudiation of the Catholic past, the mob desecrated the tombs of some of the Stewart kings and queens who had been buried there. Subsequently the bones were gathered together and sealed into a royal charnel in the abbey, where they remain safely but unimpressively housed.

James VII and II's attempts to regain his kingdoms were ineffectual. He lived for the remainder of his life in France, where as the guest of Louis XIV he maintained a shadow Court at St Germain-en-Laye. He became increasingly addicted to penitential practices, leaving his equally devout but more vigorous consort Mary of Modena to look after the political prospects of their son, Prince James Francis Edward.

🏵 From the Revolution to the Union: William and Mary and Queen Anne

William III and Mary II were crowned as joint sovereigns on 11 April 1689. William was of course technically William II of Scotland since only one previous Scottish king had borne the same name : William 'the Lion'. However, William of Orange was never officially known as William 'II and III'.

The new King and Queen were undeniably usurpers, for they had supplanted a living sovereign of indisputable legality and displaced the direct heir James Francis Edward. They were nonetheless welcomed in both Scotland and England as deliverers of the two kingdoms from the threat of 'popery'.

In Scotland, as in England, a 'Revolution Settlement' sought to redefine the relations of monarchy, Church and State. The Scottish Revolution Settlement, negotiated between April 1689 and June 1690, established Presbyterianism as the official religion of Scotland, abolished episcopacy and freed Parliament to a large extent from royal control – much against King William's will – by the abolition of the Lords of the Articles.

The Revolution Settlement was on the whole moderate and statesmanlike, but it could not be universally pleasing. The most extreme Covenanters were dissatisfied because Presbyterianism was defined on the basis of an act dating from the reign of James VI, not on that of the National Covenant of 1638. A group of disaffected sectarians therefore remained aloof from the new establishment. At the opposite extreme the defeated episcopalians tended to revert to their former loyalty, and many became supporters of the exiled James VII and his son.

The cause of James VII was by no means moribund. Catholics – principally Highlanders – episcopalians and supporters of the legitimist principle constituted a sufficiently strong 'Jacobite' party to resist King William.

The Catholic Duke of Gordon attempted to hold Edinburgh Castle in King James's name but was obliged to surrender it in June 1689. However, the following month Graham of Claverhouse, now Viscount Dundee, with an army of Highlanders, defeated King William's troops at the battle of Killiecrankie. Dundee himself was killed, and the Jacobites were unable to replace him with a commander of equal ability. They were twice defeated, at Dunkeld in August 1689 and at Cromdale in May 1690.

King William secured his success by building Fort William to establish his control over the Highlands, and he demanded an oath of allegiance from Jacobite chiefs, to be sworn by 1 January 1692.

The degree of King William's personal responsibility for what followed remains a matter of controversy. He may have accepted the advice of Sir John Dalrymple, Master of Stair, that to teach some of the Highlanders a savage object lesson might dispose the rest to abide by the oath more submissively. James VII authorized his adherents to swear the oath to William, and they duly swore. Unhappily one of them, a suitable victim for Stair's suggested purpose, was late in arriving at Fort William.

MacDonald of Glencoe, whose followers had a record of disorder as well as of Jacobitism, was disingenuously sent on to Inveraray, and did not swear his oath until 6 January. Yet he swore. If the oath had been received, as it was given, in good faith, the lateness might have been overlooked. However, Stair had selected him as an example, and King William signed the order to 'extirpate' him and his followers. It has been claimed that William may have signed without taking the trouble to read exactly what he was ordering.

The notorious 'Massacre of Glencoe' was carried out on 13 February 1692 by a force of Campbells, hereditary enemies of the MacDonalds, commanded by Captain Robert Campbell of Glenlyon who, with his men, had received several days' hospitality from the prospective victims.

Many MacDonalds escaped the massacre; some were even warned by Campbells who were disgusted by their orders. But thirty-eight men, women and children were slain, out of an intended total of 140, the victims including MacDonald of Glencoe and his wife. It was not the number massacred which aroused a sense of outrage throughout Scotland but the cold-blooded and dishonourable manner in which the whole enterprise had been planned and ordered. The reputation of King William and his government was never redeemed.

Another unhappy episode, of a very different kind – a mercantile disaster – added to his unpopularity.

After the relatively satisfactory settlement of Scotland's religious affairs which followed the Revolution, the patriotic Andrew Fletcher of Saltoun observed : 'By an unforeseen change of the genius of the nation, all their thoughts and inclinations seemed to be turned upon trade.'

In 1695 the Scottish Parliament passed an Act for a Company Trading to Africa and the Indies. The Scots were anxious to break the monopoly of the English East India Company; but the English Parliament, where the interests of the East India Company were powerfully represented, forbade English participation in the Scottish venture. The Scots were undeterred. They rethought the scheme as a colonial enterprise and planned a Scots Colony in Darien (the Isthmus of Panama) which appeared to offer singular advantages as an easy point of contact between the Atlantic and Pacific Oceans.

Unfortunately for the Scots, Darien was claimed by the Crown of Spain, and King William was desirous to remain on good terms with Spain since his enemy Louis xiv was advancing French claims to the Spanish succession.

In opposition both to English commercial interests and to the political interests of their sovereign, the Scots raised the necessary capital, and a first expedition sailed to Darien, with insufficient provisions and an unsuitable cargo, in November 1698. Two more expeditions followed and each encountered misfortune in turn. Defeated by sickness and finally overcome by Spanish hostility, very few survivors returned in 1700. For colonial failure, loss of life and financial ruin King William was blamed. The Darien disaster not only increased the Scots' dislike of William, it led to intense anti-English feeling, for the selfishness of English commercial interests was blamed almost as much as the political commitment of the King and his government.

William's attitude to Scotland during the Darien episode gives point to Fletcher of Saltoun's remark that Scotland was 'a farm managed by servants and not under the eye of the master'. William iii was not only King of Great Britain, he was an international ruler who dedicated his life to resisting the attempt of Louis xiv to dominate Europe. The large scope of his preoccupations lies outside a brief account of his reign as sovereign of Scotland; Scotland indeed received a very small proportion of his attention, and England also was of secondary importance to him. Unsurprisingly, he was never popular in either kingdom, though in England, without Glencoe or Darien to discolour his memory, his reputation stands higher. He was a man of indomitable character and great ability, respected by many people, though beloved by few.

Queen Mary, who made up for her husband's deficiency in popularity, died of smallpox in 1694. She was a devout Anglican and a devoted and unfailingly submissive wife. Beautiful in youth and charming throughout her life, she was universally mourned, not least by William, whose grief astonished many who had not suspected the depth of his feeling for her.

After her death King William's enemies made the most of the opportunities for scandal provided by the uneasy triangular relationship between the King, his lifelong friend Hans Willem Bentinck, Earl of Portland, and his young favourite Arnoud Joost van Keppel, Earl of Albemarle. King William, however, was a very secretive man, whose loves or friendships were conducted with the greatest discretion; he carried the mysteries of his private life with him to the grave.

William died in 1702. He had recognized the damage to Anglo-Scottish relations caused by conflicting interests, and to him the solution was clear. 'Nothing', said William shortly before his death, 'can contribute more to the present and future peace, security and happiness of England and Scotland than a firm and entire union between them.'

From the English viewpoint union had been growing increasingly desirable ever since the Revolution. The abolition of the Lords of the Articles had given Scotland a degree of parliamentary autonomy which made Scotland and England more separate than they had ever been since the Union of Crowns. The Darien disaster had illustrated the anomaly of two separate parliamentary states co-existing under a regal union. The early years of the next reign, which revealed greater dangers and increasing enmity, paradoxically suggested 'entire union' as the best solution.

King William, whose marriage had been childless, was succeeded by his sister-in-law, who became the last Stuart sovereign, Queen Anne. The influence of Queen Anne upon the great events of her time was peripheral by comparison with that of William. Nonetheless, she possessed a strong sense of regality. Her court

was characterized by elaborate though dully conducted ceremonial; her pleasures were simple – food, cards and hunting
occupied her leisure.

In 1683 Anne had married Prince George of Denmark, of
whom Charles II made the oft-quoted comment, 'I have tried him
drunk and I have tried him sober, and there is nothing in him.'
Anne's emotional life was dominated by passionate though essentially innocent friendships with two women : the brilliant and
forceful Sarah, Duchess of Marlborough, and her pliant supplanter, Abigail Masham. Before Queen Anne's accession at the
age of thirty-seven, the youthful prettiness which she had once
possessed had been destroyed by the effects of over-eating and
repeated child-bearing. Mary II's childlessness had a grotesquely
tragic contrast in Anne's fecundity : her eighteen pregnancies
resulted in either stillbirths or weakling children who died in
infancy. One son, William, Duke of Gloucester, an intelligent and
promising boy, reached the age of eleven, but he died in 1700.
It was then recognized that the reigning dynasty was unlikely to
produce an heir. Accordingly, since the son of James VII and II
was being brought up as a Catholic in France, in 1701 the
English Parliament passed an Act of Settlement, which declared
that the Crown should pass to the nearest Protestant heiress,
Sophia, Electress of Hanover, the grand-daughter of James VI
and I (see Genealogical Table No 5), and to her descendants.

Scotland did not automatically follow England's example. The
Scots were still debarred from participating in England's over-
seas trade, and the Scottish Parliament took the opportunity of
expressing its resentment by refusing to agree to the English
Act of Settlement. Queen Anne's first Parliament, fully aware
of the danger that Scotland might accept the Jacobite succession
and receive the support of Louis XIV, appointed commissioners
to discuss the possibility of Union. But the move was premature
and these initial negotiations broke down.

The Scottish Parliament which met in 1703, though it proved
to be the last, showed at the outset a strong spirit of independence. It passed the Act anent Peace and War, which asserted
the necessity of Scotland's consent to either, and the Wine Act,

which stated Scotland's right to continue the wine trade with France while England and France were at war. The following year it passed the Act of Security, by which Scotland repudiated the Hanoverian Succession except upon terms which secured Scotland's crown, Parliament, religion and trade against English control.

This Act, which came close to being a full assertion of Scottish sovereignty and separatism and contained an implied threat to sever the regal union, provoked the English Parliament to retaliate with the Alien Act, which required Scotland to accept the Hanoverian Succession by Christmas Day 1705, otherwise Scots would be regarded as foreigners, debarred from trade with England and subjected to a variety of legal disabilities. The Act also contained clauses inviting Scotland to consider the alternative of a 'nearer and more complete' union with England.

Under circumstances which contained an element of coercion by the country which possessed the commercial advantage, Scotland accepted the necessity for Union. Commissioners for both kingdoms were appointed. The Treaty of Union was drafted during 1706, and the two kingdoms were officially united on 1 May 1707.

The Union deprived Scotland of the status of a separate nation. Great Britain, a familiar name since 1603, became a definitive term. A new peerage of Great Britain was created to replace the separate peerages. To the new Parliament of Great Britain Scotland sent forty-five commons to join an existing 513 and sixteen lords to join an upper house of 190. In recompense for assuming a share in the responsibility for England's National Debt Scotland received an 'Equivalent' of £398,085. 10s, and the Scots were admitted to equal trading rights at home and abroad. The English coinage superseded that of Scotland, and the English Customs and Excise laws (with various temporary exemptions) became applicable in Scotland. It was agreed that the religion and the legal system of Scotland should remain unaltered.

It was evident that the commissioners had endeavoured to negotiate the Union with fairness and common sense, and it would be idle to pretend that Scotland did not derive advantages from it. But inevitably it was the anomalies and the disadvantages which were first revealed. The Scots had second thoughts, and in 1713 a motion in the House of Lords to dissolve the Union was defeated by four votes. The decision to unite and the decision to remain united were made by a few influential men. If the unrepresented people of Scotland had been consulted, there is no doubt that the Union would not have taken place. Shortly after it, Daniel Defoe reported : 'I never saw a nation so universally wild . . . it seems a perfect gangrene of the temper.' The explanation of the bitter anger is not far to seek : the Union was supposed to be a union of equal partners, but the element of subordination in it could not be concealed.

At the Union the monarchy of Scotland was merged with that of England, and on the death of Queen Anne, on 1 August 1714, the crown of the Stuarts, in ultimate fulfilment of the last words of James v, 'passed with a lass'. Her successor was the Electress Sophia's son, George i, who became King of the United Kingdom of Great Britain. It was the logical result of the Union of Crowns, though not necessarily the logical conclusion of the whole course of Scotland's history.

6

EPILOGUE:
KINGS OVER THE WATER
1701–1807

No account of the Kings and Queens of Scotland would be complete without an epilogue to conclude the story of the exiled Stuarts.

James VII and II, his son and his grandsons remained in Jacobite eyes the lawful Kings of Great Britain, albeit Kings 'over the water'. As the eighteenth century progressed, the House of Hanover became ever more firmly established. Jacobite hopes gradually faded but two principal attempts were made to bring about a Stuart restoration – in 1715 and 1745 – and in both of them Scotland played the leading part.

Prince James Francis Edward, who was taken to France when he was less than a year old, spent his childhood at the Court of his exiled parents at St Germain. William III would have been willing to adopt him as his heir, on condition of his being sent to England to be educated as a Protestant. Such a proposition was inevitably unacceptable to so ardent a convert as James VII and II, to so devout a Catholic as Mary of Modena and to their protector King Louis XIV.

On 6 September 1701 James VII and II died at St Germain. Louis XIV visited him on his deathbed and took leave of him with the words '*Adieu, mon frère, le meilleur, le plus outragé des hommes*' ('Farewell, my brother, the best and the most ill-used of men'). Deeply moved by the fate of a Catholic sovereign who had lost his throne for his religion, the French King immediately proclaimed Prince James Francis Edward as James 'VIII of Scotland and III of England'. Though Louis had been obliged to acknowledge William III as *de facto* King of Great Britain, he had continued to recognize James VII and II as King *de jure*. He gave the same recognition to James's son for reasons both of principle and of policy. In the young James 'VIII and III' he possessed a political pawn of great value, who could be used against the established government of England whenever the policy of France required it.

When James 'VIII and III' was proclaimed King at St Germain, he was thirteen years old. His religious training had given him a deep faith which was untinged by his father's fanaticism. He had received a good education : he was trilingual in English, French and Italian and capable of corresponding in Latin. He was an elegant dancer and a fine horseman and he excelled at both shooting and fencing. He fulfilled the lingering renaissance ideal of a King who displayed a well-balanced range of intellectual and physical accomplishments.

His good looks were much admired. He had the height and the aquiline features which characterized the Stuarts, and he had inherited the black eyes and hair of his Italian mother. From his dark colouring derived his nickname, 'the Bonnie Black Laddie', which provided the title of a song written in his honour :

My Laddie can fight, my Laddie can sing,
He's fierce like the North Wind, yet soft as the Spring,
His soul was designed for no less than a King,
Such greatness shines in my Black Laddie.

Though their young King was a worthy object for the admiration of his supporters, there was a negative side to his character which provided a basis for the contemptuous and dismissive attitude assumed by his enemies. Though he possessed a profound belief in his own kingship and was resolved to gain the throne of Great Britain if he could, he was not a natural optimist. Though he was admired, and in later years even reverenced, by those who knew him well, he could not convert waverers or inspire strangers with a contagion of enthusiasm. He lacked magnetism. As he grew older, he became increasingly austere and withdrawn. The element of fatalism in his nature enabled him to display admirable fortitude in adversity, yet he seemed almost to have courted adversity by his determination to be prepared for it.

James's chance of gaining his kingdoms by inheritance seemed gone forever when the English Act of Settlement was passed in 1701 in favour of the House of Hanover. His first attempt to win them by force took place in March 1708, when a French fleet brought him within sight of Scotland. An encounter with English warships and a violent storm deterred the French commander, who had orders not to let James endanger his life. Despite the arguments and entreaties of the young King, the Frenchman refused to let him land, and the fleet sailed back to France. If James had landed in Scotland in 1708, when anti-Union feeling was very strong, he would have had a fair chance of regaining at least his northern kingdom, but that chance was lost.

On his return to France, knowing that another attempt might be long deferred, he sought Louis xiv's permission to gain the military experience which he needed with the French army. For the next few years he took part in King Louis's wars under the incognito of the Chevalier de Saint George. He distinguished himself by his courage at the battles of Oudenarde and Malplaquet.

In 1713, when Anglo-French hostilities were ended by the Treaty of Utrecht, Louis xiv was obliged to recognize the Hanoverian succession and to abandon his patronage of 'the Pretender'.

James saved the French King the embarrassment of being obliged to request him to leave France by withdrawing to Lorraine, where he stayed as the Duke of Lorraine's guest at Bar-le-Duc. Mary of Modena remained at St Germain, to look after her son's interests in France as best she could. She died in 1718.

From 1713 onwards, James's greatest difficulty in organizing attempts at restoration was that of communications. Attenuated contacts with Britain and the increasing hazard of intercepted correspondence both contributed to the ultimate failure of the Jacobites.

James had a last chance of peaceful succession to his kingdoms on the death of Queen Anne in 1714, when once again he could have secured the throne by conversion to Protestantism. But he was not prepared to compromise his own integrity, though he had notions of religious toleration which were in advance of his times. As he wrote some years later: 'I am a Catholic, but I am a King, and subjects of whatever religion they may be, have an equal right to be protected. I am a King, but ... I am not an apostle. I am not bound to convert my people otherwise than by my example, nor to show apparent partiality to Catholics, which would only serve to injure them later.'

Such a level-headed attitude would have saved the throne of James VII and II, but it would not serve to regain it for James 'VIII and III'. The Hanoverian succession took place without a rising in James's favour.

The rising of 1715, though it was intended to take advantage of the personal unpopularity of George I, was essentially too late. It was also too late to make use of Louis XIV's almost paternal affection for James; the King of France, after a reign of seventy-two years, died on 1 September 1715. In the meantime the rising had begun in Scotland.

John Erskine, sixth Earl of Mar, whose contemporaries scornfully nicknamed him 'Bobbing John', was the inadequate leader of the rising. Pro-Union in 1707, and one of the signatories of the Treaty, he had become disillusioned with the Union and dissatisfied with his own rewards. He turned Jacobite.

On 26 August the Earl held a great hunting-party in Braemar, which provided the excuse for the initial gathering of armed men. On 6 September he proclaimed King James VIII and III, raised the royal standard and made a bid for popular support by denouncing the Union.

The first response was impressive. It provided Mar with an army of five thousand Jacobite Highlanders, which on 16 September captured Perth. There Mar remained to recruit more supporters and to await the arrival of James. The Jacobite army continued to grow until it reached twelve thousand.

In October a force of fifteen hundred Jacobites led by Mackintosh of Borlum crossed the Forth and attempted to surprise Edinburgh. Turned aside by the Duke of Argyll who commanded a government force, Borlum marched south and joined forces with Jacobites from the south-west of Scotland who had risen under Lord Kenmure, and English Jacobites from Northumberland led by Lord Derwentwater. They invaded England by the western route, hoping to gain more support on their way, only to be defeated at Preston on 14 November.

In the meantime, the inactivity of the Earl of Mar had given Argyll chance to gather sufficient reinforcements to meet him in battle. Mar, who had lost all his initial advantage, met Argyll at Sheriffmuir, near Stirling. The battle, which took place on 13 November, was claimed by both sides as a victory.

Lack of communication explained the non-appearance of James. Informed too late at every stage of the proceedings, he had not left Lorraine until October. In France he had received the news of Sheriffmuir, reported as a Jacobite victory. James, who was obliged to cross France in disguise, had great difficulty in leaving it at all. Eventually he reached Scotland, suffering from ague and scarcely recovered from measles. He landed at Peterhead on 22 December.

Mar's army had been dwindling from desertion as it awaited the arrival of James, while Argyll's had been steadily reinforced. The defeat of the Jacobites was held off only by heavy snow. James was escorted south to meet his adherents at Perth and ostensibly to be crowned at Scone. But he failed to fire the enthusiasm of an army which was already sensible of defeat. The crown, which was to have been made from jewels offered by Jacobite ladies, was never set on his head. The advance of Argyll put an end to an already doomed enterprise. James left Scotland again, in ignominious retreat, at the beginning of February. He returned to France accompanied by Mar, and his supporters scattered to save themselves as best they could.

Many Jacobites captured at Preston, including Lords Kenmure and Derwentwater, were executed, and the government ordered the disarming of the Highlands. The Jacobite Highlanders did not regard their defeat as final; they surrendered old swords and obsolete firearms and kept their best weapons to fight another day.

James accepted his defeat with stoicism. '[I] . . . would have thought myself to some degree content', he wrote, 'if I were alone in my misfortune, but the death and misfortune of others . . . pierces my heart.' His enemies ridiculed him as 'Old Mr Melancholy'.

After the failure of the '15 James was no longer able to find

refuge in Lorraine. He was driven to seek asylum in papal territory at Avignon, to which he went reluctantly, knowing that
closer relations with the Papacy would cost him many Protestant
supporters.

Despite failure in Scotland, Jacobite hopes were rapidly translated into action again. Promises of Spanish support encouraged
James to visit Spain himself in spring 1719, but the results were
disappointing : a small-scale invasion of Scotland was defeated in
Glenshiel on 10 June, James's thirty-first birthday.

James had hoped to leave Spain for Scotland, instead he left it
to return to Italy, for further promises of help proved ground-
less. However, he returned in the hope of some happiness at last,
for during the previous year he had negotiated his marriage,
and his bride awaited him in Italy. She was Princess Maria
Clementina Sobieska, the grand-daughter of John III Sobieski,
King of Poland. She was also the god-daughter of Pope
Clement XI, a connection scarcely calculated to increase James's
popularity in Britain.

Clementina was an enchantingly pretty girl of seventeen, tiny
in stature, vivacious yet dignified. She was intensely devout, to
an extent which within a few years suggested religious mania
rather than sanctity.

A proxy marriage had taken place while James was in Spain.
The Nuptial Mass was celebrated in the Cathedral of Monte-
fiascone on 1 September 1719. After his marriage James reconciled himself to a close connection with the Pope, the last
powerful ally on whom he could rely. With Clementina he
settled in Rome, in the Palazzo Muti, the gift of Pope Clement.
A sombre, intrigue-ridden Court formed itself around him.

The first son of James 'VIII and III' and Queen Clementina was
born on 31 December 1720. He was Prince Charles Edward,
whose adventurous early life was to create the legendary figure
of 'Bonnie Prince Charlie'. The legend almost obscures the true
lineaments of the Prince, who was a man possessed of heroic
qualities and perhaps rather more than his fair share of human
failings. His birth seemed almost messianic, for it was reported

that on the night of 31 December a new star appeared and a violent storm ravaged the city of Hanover. The Jacobites had no doubt of the message of these portents, and the central purpose of Charles's upbringing was to prepare him to effect the restoration of his family. Many years later he commissioned a medal which bore his profile and on the reverse the legend *Amor et Spes Britanniae* (the Love and Hope of Britain) – such was the image of himself with which he grew up.

In 1725 James and Clementina produced a second son, Prince Henry Benedict. The Stuart line seemed safely perpetuated.

Both boys were healthy, intelligent and promising, both were strikingly good-looking, and it seemed only proper that the elder should outshine the younger in almost all accomplishments. Henry was the better scholar, and even in childhood he showed signs of having inherited his mother's piety. Charles was athletic, and early in life he was described as having an 'overmastering passion for the profession of arms'. He was a natural linguist who grew up speaking Italian, French and English. In adolescence he was reported as knowing some Spanish, and in 1745 he acquired spoken Gaelic with remarkable facility. He enjoyed what came easily to him, but his 'Governor' Lord Dunbar complained, 'it is impossible to get him to apply to any study as he ought to do . . . by which means the Latin goes ill on.'

Dunbar was a Protestant, but Charles also had a Catholic tutor, Sir Thomas Sheridan, who was in charge of his religious instruction. Clementina quarrelled bitterly with her husband over Charles's education, for she was terrified of the contagion of James's liberal ideas. Left to herself, she would have had her son not only a Catholic but as bigoted a Catholic as possible. Fortunately James prevailed. But there were other causes of trouble. Clementina resented her husband's friendship with his faithful supporter John Hay, Earl of Inverness, and she groundlessly suspected him of adultery with Lady Inverness. For a time she left the Palazzo Muti and took refuge in a convent. Domestic discord was increased by the claustrophobic atmosphere of the Jacobite Court: while some courtiers sided with the King and

others with the Queen, quarrels multiplied, and the reconciliation of the principals seemed almost impossible. Reason, however, prevailed at last, and Clementina returned, but she had
undermined her health with self-imposed austerities which were
far from reasonable. Excessive fasting probably hastened her
early death in 1735.

Charles was grief-stricken at his mother's death, yet he was
ambitious and resilient. The future soon claimed his attention.
In 1737, to complete his education, he was sent on a 'grand tour'
of Italian Courts. Everywhere he went he was praised and admired, and his journey became something like a triumphal pro-
gress. In Venice he was received with so much enthusiasm that
when the news reached London, George II's government was
sufficiently offended to expel the Venetian resident from
England. Prince Charles Edward had ceased to be a boy in Italy;
he had become a figure upon the stage of the world.

In 1740 the death of the Emperor Charles VI and the accession
of Maria Theresa inaugurated the War of the Austrian Succession: a great European convulsion offered the Prince the
chance for which his whole life had been a preparation. Once
again Stuart hopes centred upon French assistance, while France
prepared to make use of the Stuarts in the interests of French
policy. In January 1744 France was preparing an invasion of
England. A force of ten thousand men and a fleet of transport
ships was assembled at Dunkirk under the command of the
Maréchal de Saxe. The Prince left Rome in disguise and
travelled incognito to join the expedition. In a spirit of high
optimism he took leave of his father with the words : 'I go, Sire,
in search of three Crowns, which I doubt not but to have the
honour of laying at your Majesty's feet.'

Disaster might well have quenched Charles's initial optimism,
for in March Saxe's invasion force was scattered and largely
destroyed by storms, and the projected invasion was abandoned.
Charles waited upon further help from France, as his father had
waited in Spain in 1719. When 1745 opened with a French
victory at Fontenoy over combined English and Dutch forces,
the Prince tried to persuade Louis XV to mount a new invasion of

England. But the French King had begun to doubt that an invasion would be supported by a Jacobite rising.

Charles was determined not to return to Italy only to report broken promises. He had already reached the conclusion, as he wrote to his father, that 'if it is impossible to transport the necessary troops into England, the best will be to turn our thoughts to Scotland'.

The rising of 1745 had its inception in the optimism of Prince Charles Edward and in his conviction that Scottish and English Jacobites were merely awaiting his arrival to rise as one man. He did not inform his father of his audacious resolve to go to Scotland alone, if need be, until it was too late for James to stop him.

Charles left France on 5 July with two ships, one of which was intercepted by an English warship and forced to return. On 23 July Charles landed on Eriskay in the Outer Hebrides. He had seven companions – 'the Seven Men of Moidart'. The extraordinary legend of 'Bonnie Prince Charlie' had begun.

The response of the chiefs whom the Prince had summoned to meet him was less enthusiastic than he had expected. Two refused to join him, and a third, MacDonald of Boisdale, advised him to go home. He replied, 'I am come home, Sir, and will entertain no notion at all of returning to that place from whence I came, for I am persuaded my faithful Highlanders will stand by me.' He was always capable of a dramatic turn of phrase, and on the whole his expectation was right, for there was a great deal of Jacobite sentiment in the Highlands for him to draw upon. The leading Gaelic poet of the day had prepared the way for him:

> *Thig thar lear le gaoith anear oirnn*
> *Toradh deal ar dòchais,*
> *Le 'mhilte fear's le armaibh geal,*
> *Prionns' ullamh, mear, 's è do-chaisgt';*
> *Mac Righ Seumas, Teàrlach Stiùbhart,*
> *Oighre 'chrùin th' air fogradh;*
> *Gun dean gach Breatunnach làn-ùmhlachd*
> *Air an glùn d'a mhòrachd.*

⌈With eastern winds will come o'er-seas
    One we've keenly hoped for,
With many men and shining arms,
    Ready, quick, unhindered;
Prince Charles Stuart, the son of James,
    The crown's heir from his exile.
Let every Briton homage do
    On bended knees before him.⌉

Despite his lack of 'many men and shining arms', Charles rapidly gained support when he reached the mainland. Two powerful chiefs joined him: MacDonald of Clanranald and Cameron of Lochiel. Their adherence gave him a force of about nine hundred clansmen. On 19 August 1745, in Glenfinnan at the head of Lochshiel, the Prince raised his standard and proclaimed his father King James VIII and III. He marched south and the successful first phase of the rising began. The Jacobite army grew by the way; Perth fell, and the Prince entered Edinburgh on 17 September. King James VIII and III was again proclaimed at the Mercat Cross. The Prince rode in triumph to Holyroodhouse, where he held Court during the ensuing weeks.

On 21 September Charles gained his first victory, over English forces commanded by Sir John Cope, at Prestonpans, just outside Edinburgh. This victory was the high point of Charles's success. After it he delayed too long in Edinburgh, hoping that Louis XV would be encouraged to send reinforcements. Arms and money came indeed but no soldiers. Charles was convinced that if his gains in Scotland were not swiftly followed by an invasion of England, they would be as swiftly lost again, especially as Marshal Wade had arrived at Newcastle and was only awaiting reinforcements before marching north. Charles decided to invade England, although his army, through lack of active Jacobitism in the Lowlands, had grown to only about eight thousand men.

Early in November the Prince began his advance on London. His boldness caused such terror that George II was reported to be preparing to retire to Hanover. However, his son William

Augustus, Duke of Cumberland, was raising a second army to take the field against the Prince.

On the march south English Jacobites did not flock to the Prince's standard as he had hoped. By 4 December he had reached Derby, and his army had been reinforced only by three hundred men from Manchester. One hundred and thirty miles from London the Prince's officers lost their nerve. Headed by the Lieutenant General Lord George Murray, an able but cautious commander, they urged the Prince to turn north again, to consolidate his gains in Scotland.

Hitherto Charles had won his successes by incredible audacity, and it is just possible that audacity might have won London, though only the doubtful possibilities of massive reinforcement from France and a general Jacobite rising could have held it. However, Charles knew that to turn back to Scotland looked like a recognition of ultimate defeat.

Once the wisdom of boldness had become subject to doubt, the Prince's officers found his boldness frankly alarming. Led by Lord George Murray, they demanded that military decisions be subject to a 'Committee of Commanders'. Charles resisted bitterly and was overruled. The committee was formed, and resolved upon retreat.

By 20 December the Jacobite army was back in Scotland, and the northward march, urged by Lord George Murray, continued. In January 1746 the Prince won his last success when his Highlanders put to flight a slightly larger English force under General Hawley, at Falkirk. Charles wished to take advantage of this slight success by laying siege to Stirling but once again his officers urged him to withdraw farther north. French reinforcements were still talked of, though scarcely to be expected.

The Prince established his headquarters at Inverness, where inactivity rapidly lowered the Highlanders' morale. In the meantime, the Duke of Cumberland was assembling his army at Aberdeen. Knowing that time was on his side, Cumberland ensured that his preparations should be thorough rather than speedy. It was not until 16 April that the decisive battle was fought on Culloden Moor, near Inverness.

Culloden was the end of the Prince's hopes, for Cumberland's artillery won the day and inflicted terrible slaughter upon the Highlanders. Cumberland, however, gained no glory by his victory : his atrocities committed upon the wounded and the prisoners after the battle gained him the name of 'the Butcher Cumberland'. It was an unhappy thing for the Prince's subsequent reputation that he survived the battle, though posterity has taken a kinder view of his reluctant flight from the field than one of his embittered supporters who remarked, 'There you go for a damned cowardly Italian.'

Culloden was followed by one of the most famous manhunts in history. From April to September Charles was a fugitive with a price of £30,000 on his head. His attempts to evade capture, and to find one of the many French ships which were sent to save him, took him from the mainland to North and South Uist, to Skye and back to the mainland once again. Highlanders and Islanders contemptuously ignored the reward, and the Prince was helped on his way with courage and ingenuity by many people besides the best remembered, Flora MacDonald. At last, on 19 September, the Prince found the French brig *L'Heureux*, which landed him safely in France on 1 October.

Charles did not immediately recognize his defeat as final. He seems to have returned to France expecting that he had only to reappear in person and demand Louis xv's help in order to receive it. His optimism died very hard. At last he was forced to face the reality of the situation : his heroic failure might be admired and pitied, but France would not risk anything to help him recoup it.

Gradually he learned of the price which his adherents were paying for the failure of the '45. The sufferings of the Highlanders did not end with the atrocities which followed Culloden. The civilian population suffered cruelly in the devastation which Cumberland's troops carried out as a deliberate policy of reprisal and the surviving participants in the rising inevitably suffered the rigours of the law. One hundred and twenty were executed, about one thousand were deported and several hundred died as victims of the filthy conditions of their imprisonment. The

Disarming Act of 1746, which was carried out with much more thoroughness than that which had followed the rising of 1715, and the prohibition of the pipes and of Highland dress, were intended to pacify a disaffected area and to eliminate the characteristics of the Highland way of life in which Jacobitism had flourished. The unintended result was that Jacobitism took on all the romance of a persecuted cause, and Prince Charles Edward became the central figure of a legend which enshrined his heroic qualities and forgave him the unhappy consequences of his gamble to restore the House of Stuart.

The last years of the exiled Stuarts were far from legendary.

Prince Henry, a greater realist than his brother, took Holy Orders in 1747 and was immediately made a Cardinal, which gave him a dignity in the Church befitting the dignity of royal blood. As he was titular Duke of York, Henry was thereafter usually known as Cardinal York.

Sir Horace Mann, the English resident in Florence, commented : 'Cardinal Stuart by putting on the cowl has done more to extinguish his party than would have been effected by putting to death many thousands of deluded followers.' This was exactly his brother's view. Charles did not reflect that Henry had shown some wisdom as well as some self-interest in preferring a career in the Church to an unemployed existence as a shadow of royalty. He saw only a blow to the cause, which he would not admit had already received its death-blow. His anger with his brother continued unabated for eighteen years.

Bitterly angry with both his brother and his father, who had supported Henry, Charles remained in France, steadfastly refusing to return to Rome. Autumn 1748 witnessed the end of the War of the Austrian Succession, and by the terms of the Treaty of Aix-la-Chapelle Charles was obliged to leave France. As a public protest against what he considered unjust and ungenerous treatment, he refused to go. Louis xv was reluctantly obliged to take an action which he had genuinely wished to avoid : Charles was arrested in December but released upon his promise to leave France immediately. He sought refuge in Avignon, as his father had done in less humiliating circumstances, many years before.

The effects upon the character of the Prince of disappointment, frustration, humiliation and a sense of guilt, were slow, but the erosion of all these destructive influences showed itself insistently with the passage of years.

In 1750 Charles secretly visited England and was received into the Anglican Church, probably with the hope of counteracting the effect upon the English Jacobites of his brother's becoming a Cardinal. From 1750 onwards Charles almost ceased to communicate with his father, and in the interests of concealing his apostasy he refused to revisit Rome. (He returned to the Church of Rome after his father's death.)

James was anxious to see his son married, but Charles wrote to explain his reluctance: 'I think our family have had sufferings enough that will always hinder me to marry as long as in misfortune.' But the truth was that Charles was living with a girl named Clementina Walkinshaw, who had borne him a daughter, named Charlotte, in 1753. The affair was unhappy. Charles quarrelled with his mistress and began drinking heavily. In 1760 Clementina left him and, taking Charlotte with her, went to live in a convent in France.

Charles's unhappy condition was made worse when someone told James of his son's apostasy. James wrote to him: 'I am far from dissuading you to seek a Temporal Kingdom . . . and it is manifestly for the good of our country that it should return under the dominion of our family. But . . . what will avail you all the Kingdoms of the world . . . if you lose your soul? I am in agonies for you, my dear son. . . .'

Many times James tried to persuade his son to give up his 'indecent, wandering life' and come to Rome, but the Prince detested being cast in the role of the prodigal, and he continued to refuse. At last, in 1765, informed that his father was dying, he agreed to come. He set out, but arrived too late. James 'VIII and III' died on 1 January 1766.

James lay in state in the church of the Santi Apostoli opposite the Palazzo Muti, wearing the crown which he had never worn in life, and was given a King's funeral in St Peter's.

To loyal Jacobites Prince Charles Edward now became King 'Charles III'. However, the Stuart cause was politically dead, and Pope Clement XIII refused 'Charles III' the recognition of *de jure* sovereignty which had always been granted to his father.

Injured as he was by what he regarded as an unpardonable slight, Charles could only solace himself by insisting upon private recognition of his regality. He now acknowledged that it was his duty as a King to marry and secure the shadowy succession of his family. In 1772 he found a suitable bride, Princess Louise of Stolberg. She was a handsome girl of twenty who enjoyed the adulation of the remaining Jacobite courtiers and the pleasure of signing herself 'Louise R'; but she found little to delight her in a fifty-two-year-old husband who was cruelly described by Sir Horace Mann as 'insupportable in stench and temper'. The same writer remarked that Louise had 'paid dearly for the dregs of royalty'. Louise herself apparently thought so, for in 1780 she left her husband and went to live with her lover, the Italian poet Alfieri. In 1784 Charles granted her a legal separation. The marriage had failed in its principal purpose: there were no children.

Charles was now lonely, depressed and prematurely old. He remembered his daughter Charlotte, whom he had last seen in 1760. He took a decision which illuminated the last years of his life with a little happiness. He sent for her.

The charming, intelligent and strong-minded Charlotte delighted her father. He legitimated her and created her Duchess of Albany. Her slightly disciplinarian affection did him a great deal of good; she put an end to his drunken depression and encouraged him to make up his quarrel with Cardinal York.

The Cardinal was at first far from pleased by the legitimation of Charlotte, which possibly represented a threat to his own tenuous rights of succession. But the rivalry was too unreal to provide much basis for a quarrel, and few could resist the Duchess of Albany's charm. The Cardinal was soon referring to her as his 'Royal Niece'.

Charles died on 30 January 1788. Since the Pope had not recognized him as King of Great Britain, he could not be given a

King's funeral in Rome as his father had been. The Cardinal therefore provided one for him in his own Cathedral of Frascati, where 'Charles III' was buried with full royal honours.

Far away in Scotland one man at least thought of Charlotte as the heiress to the throne. Robert Burns wrote:

> My heart is wae and unco wae
>   To think upon the raging sea
> That roars between the gardens green
>   An' the bonnie lass of Albany. . . .

> We'll daily pray, we'll nightly pray
>   On bended knees most fervently,
> The time may come with pipe and drum
>   We'll welcome home Fair Albany.

The time did not come; indeed, it could never have come. Charlotte died the year after her father, at the age of thirty-six.

Cardinal York had always taken pleasure in the grandeur derived from his royal blood, and he enjoyed the shadowy kingship, equally gratifying and undemanding, which came to him after his brother's death. He assumed the title of 'Henry IX'. Though Scotland had never had a King Henry, he did not trouble to style himself 'Henry I of Scotland and IX of England', as he might have done if he had ever visited the different kingdoms from which he derived his kingship.

His existence as a magnificent Prince of the Church ended in 1799 with the Napoleonic invasion of Italy. Reduced to poverty, he was grateful to accept the pension which George III magnanimously offered him. He died in 1807 and was buried in St Peter's, together with his father and his brother, whose remains had been removed there in 1800.

The white marble tomb carved by Canova contains the bones of the last members of Scotland's royal line – James 'VIII and III', 'Charles III' and 'Henry IX' – far from Scotland in body and spirit, but unforgotten.

APPENDIX:
THE STEWARTS AS POETS

In the course of this book several references have been made to poetry written by Kings and Queens of the House of Stewart, and two quotations have been given from the poems of James I and Mary, Queen of Scots. Some readers, however, may wish for further information on Stewart poetry, and accordingly this appendix offers a brief section on each of the royal poets: James I, James V, Mary, Queen of Scots, Henry, Lord Darnley and James VI and I.

1 James I

As previously mentioned, it was in 1423 that James I fell in love with Lady Joan Beaufort, an experience which he described in his long poem *The Kingis Quair* (*The King's Book*). It is supposed to have been written during the last year of his imprisonment, though upon internal evidence, it was completed after his release.

On the basis of his achievement as the author of one great poem, James I has won the reputation of one of the most distinguished courtly poets of his age. As a type of poem, *The Kingis Quair* belongs to an already established medieval poetic tradition, and its formative influences can be found in Chaucer, and ultimately in *Le Roman de La Rose* of Guillaume de Lorris and Jehan de Meun. However, James I's poem differs from its predecessors in that it is not merely an allegory or conventional dream-vision but a retelling, within the terms of contemporary literary convention, of the author's experience.

The King begins his poem by describing himself as suffering from insomnia, and consoling himself by reading Boethius (who wrote *De Consolatione Philosophiae* in prison), and meditating upon the fickleness of fortune. He laments his captive existence:

Quhare as in ward full oft I wold bewaille
My dedely lyf, full of peyne and penance,
*Saing ryght thus, quhat have I gilt to faille**
My fredome in this world and my plesance?
Sen every wight has thereof suffisance,
That I behold, and I a creature
Put from all this – hard is myn aventure!

The lamentation ends when the King goes to the window and looks down on the garden below. There nightingales are singing : James describes them and quotes the imagined words of their song :

And on the smallë grenë twistis sat
The lytill suetë nightingale, and song
So loud and clere, the ympnis consecrat
Off lufis use, now soft, now loud among,
That all the gardyng and the wallis rong
Ryght of thair song, and on the copill next
Off thair swete armony, and lo the text:
'Worschippe, ye that loveris bene, this may,
For of your blisse the kalendis are begonne,
And sing with us, away, winter away!
Come, somer, come the suete sesoun and sonne!
Awake for schame, that have your hevynis wonne!
And amorously lift up your hedis all,
Thank lufe† that list you to his merci call.'

The meditation upon love which follows precedes the appearance in the early morning of the lady with whom James falls in love at first sight. His joy at seeing her changes to despair when she leaves the garden. This description is followed by the conventional visionary portion of the poem in which James imagines himself transported in sleep to the Court of Venus, and his hymn to the goddess of love is one of the most exquisite verses of the whole poem :

* What have I done that I should deserve to lose.   † love.

O Venus clere, of goddis stellifyit,
To quhom I yeld homage and sacrifis,
Fro this day forth your grace be magnfyit,
That me ressavit have in suich wise
To lyve under your law and do servis;
Now help me furth, and for your merci lede
My hert to rest, that deis nere for drede.

Venus promises to assist James in his love. She gives him Good Hope to be his guide, by whom he is led before Minerva, who enjoins him to love with truth and virtue. Good Hope then leads him to the goddess Fortune, who bids him climb upon her wheel. Thus favoured by Fortune, he awakes. The poem ends with a reference to his recovery of freedom, which brings him 'To bliss with her that is my soveraigne'.

The Kingis Quair is the only poem definitely attributable to James I. It is not, however, the work of an occasional versifier. The poet and historian William Drummond of Hawthornden, writing in the seventeenth century, stated that 'He wrote many verses both Latin and English, of which many are yet extant.' If they were correctly attributed, it is a great misfortune that they have disappeared in the course of the last three hundred years.

2 James V

When James V was a child, his 'Master Usher' and later 'Master of the Household' was Sir David Lindsay of the Mount, the poet, satirist and dramatist who became Lord Lyon King of Arms. We have Lindsay's word that James V was a poet, for James challenged Lindsay to a 'flyting' – a popular courtly entertainment in late medieval and Renaissance Scotland, in which two poets would exchange coruscating and frequently indelicate abuse in verse.

It appears from Lindsay's reply to James's verses, which have not survived, that James had accused Lindsay of sluggishness in the pursuit of love. Lindsay's reply accuses the King of over-enthusiasm in the pursuit of it and reproaches him for the rape of a servant girl who had first fled from him and then sought to preserve her virtue by emptying a brewing-vat over his head, before being forced to surrender in a pool of beer. Lindsay commented :

> Would God the lady that lovit you best
> Had seen you there lie swettering like twa swine.*

These lines may rather prove that, within the conventions of flyting, Lindsay was permitted remarkable freedom of expression, than that James v, indiscriminate pursuer of women though he was, necessarily participated in such an incident. There is no knowing. Neither is there any knowing whether the surviving poem attributed to James can confidently be accepted as his work or not. However, it is a well-established tradition that he wrote *Christis Kirk on the Green*, a long and lively account of a rustic kermesse which deteriorates into a free-for-all. It is written in a stanza form much used in Scottish poetry, which appears to have originated in the anonymous medieval poem *Peblis to the Play*, to which reference is made in the fourth line of the first verse of *Christis Kirk on the Green*, perhaps by way of acknowledgment :

> Was never in Scotland hard nor seen
> Sic dancing nor deray,
> Nather in Falkland on the green,
> Nor Peblis to the play,
> As was of wooeris as I ween
> At Christis Kirk on ane day.
> There comes our Kittie weshen clean
> In her new kirtill of gray,
>   Full gay,
> At Christis Kirk on the green.

There are two views on this poem : the first, that it is a true example of folk poetry; and the second, that it is a courtly satire of rustic life. The latter view would accord more appropriately with the theory of royal authorship, though the former is not

* Wallowing like two pigs.

altogether incompatible with James v's own character as a folklore-figure in the guise of the 'Gudeman o' Ballengeich'.

3 *Mary, Queen of Scots*

As a result of her upbringing at the Court of France, French was Queen Mary's first language. Most of her poems were written in French and a few in Italian and Latin.

In the nineteenth century quite a large corpus of verses was attributed to Mary, but recent research has cast doubt upon the authenticity of some of them. The French song *Adieu, plaisant pays de France*, long ascribed to Mary, is now known to have been written by an eighteenth-century Frenchman, Quercy de Merlon. And as long ago as 1907, Mrs P. Stewart-Mackenzie Arbuthnot, who compiled *Queen Mary's Book*, recorded some doubts on the authenticity of *En mon triste et doux chant*, the poem of lament for François II attributed to the Queen. The notorious 'Casket Letters', by which Mary's enemies tried to establish her responsibility for the murder of Darnley, have always been of controversial authenticity, and together with them the accompanying sequence of poor quality French sonnets supposedly addressed to Bothwell.

As Ronsard's pupil, Mary became an occasional poet of some merit; happily for her reputation, the poems indisputably attributable to her are better than those which have been discarded or are in doubt.

Mary's sonnet to Elizabeth I of England has already been quoted on p. 85. During her imprisonment in England, Mary wrote a number of poems lamenting her fate and invoking the consolations of religion. Two sonnets are here translated from the original French:

I

What am I, alas, what purpose has my life?
I nothing am, a corpse without a heart,
A useless shade, a victim of sad strife,
One who lives yet, and wishes to depart.

My enemies, no envy hold for me;
My spirit has no taste for greatness now.
Sorrow consumes me in extreme degree,
Your hatred shall be satisfied, I vow.
And you, my friends, you who have held me dear,
Reflect that I, lacking both health and fortune,
Cannot aspire to any great deed here.
Welcome, therefore, my ultimate misfortune.
And pray that when affliction ends my story,
Then I may have some share in Heaven's glory.

II

O Lord and King of Heaven my prayer receive,
And let it with your holy will accord;
For only by the grace I have implored
May I maintain the faith which I believe.
Laggard in faith, O Lord, to you I cleave,
Weary already, my frail willpower ailing;
Grant me your strength, Lord, for my strength is failing,
That conquest of my fate I may achieve.
Your will, Lord, is to reign within my heart:
O come to it, and nevermore depart!
And banish from it worldly love and hate;
Let good and ill my actions regulate.
Thus only, Lord, may I receive your grace,
In faith and penitence behold your face.*

The last poem attributed to Mary is a rhymed Latin prayer, traditionally supposed to have been written on the night before her execution. Lady Antonia Fraser, in her recent biography, has cast doubt on it because Mary had so many affairs to settle in the little time allowed her that it seems unlikely that she would have been able to give time to composing the prayer. The possibility remains that Mary might have written it at some other time during her imprisonment, since it is a prayer for liberty not necessarily to be obtained through death. Its authorship, however, must be regarded as under question.

* Author's translations.

O Domine Deus,
Speravi in Te.
O care mi Jesu,
Nunc libera me.
In dura catena,
In misera poena,
Desidero Te.
Languendo, gemendo,
Et genuflectendo,
Adoro, imploro,
Ut liberes me.

[O Lord God,
I have hoped in Thee.
Beloved Jesus,
Now set me free.
In cruel chains,
In bitter pains,
I have longed for Thee.
Now languishing
In sorrow sore,
Upon my knees
I thee implore
That Thou wilt
Grant me liberty.]

4 Henry Stuart, Lord Darnley

The verses written by Mary's unfortunate consort Lord Darnley belong entirely to the tradition of Scottish courtly verse, which suggests that his upbringing in England had been that of an exiled Scot rather than an anglicized one.

The ensuing quotation is from a love lyric, usually supposed to have been addressed to the Queen, but equally likely to have been written for some other lady:

The tutour for hir maik
mair dule may nocht indure

nor I do for hir saik,
evin hir, quha hes in cure
my hart, quhilk salbe sure
in service to the deid
unto that lady pure,
the well of womanheid.

Schaw, schedull, to that sweit
my pairt so permanent
that no mirth quhill we meit
sall caus me be content,
bot still my hairt lament
in sorrowfull siching soir
till time scho be present.
Fairweill. I say no moir.

[The turtle-dove does not suffer more sorrow for her mate than I do for the sake of the lady who has my heart in her keeping. Until death, my heart shall be dedicated to the service of that chaste lady who is the very fount of womanhood. Go, my verse, and show that sweet creature that the part I play is lasting. Show her that no mirth shall give me joy until we meet, but that my heart will continue to lament, sorrowfully sighing, until she is present again. Farewell. I say no more.]

Darnley also wrote, and addressed to the Queen, a poem of *Advice to a Prince* (i.e. a ruler), which contains the conventional sentiments of the period. They are sentiments which, had he himself acted upon them, might have brought his career to a less savage end than murder at Kirk o' Field :

Be governor baith guid and gratious,
Be leill and luifand to thy liegis all,
Be large of fredome and nothing desyrous,
Be just to pure, for onything may fall.
Be ferme of faith and constant as ane wall,

Be reddye evir to stanche evill and discord,
Be cheratabill, and sickertye thou sall
Be bowsome ay to knaw thy god and lord. . . .

Be to rebellis strong as lyoun eik,
Be ferce to follow thame quhair evir thai found;
Be to thy liegemen bayth soft and meik,
Be thair succor and help thame haill and sound.
Be knaw thy cure and caus quhy thow was cround.
Be besye evir, that justice be nocht smord.
Be blyith in hart, thir wordis oft expound;
Be bowsum ay to knaw thy god and lord.

[Be a good and a gracious ruler; be loyal and loving to all
your subjects. Be generous in all things and never covetous.
Be just to the poor, for as you sow, so shall you reap. Be
steadfast in religion and as unalterable as a wall of stone.
Always be on your guard against all evil and disorder. Be
charitable, and then assuredly you will have humility, and
know God. . . . But likewise, be as strong as a lion towards
rebels; pursue them fiercely, wherever they may be. Be soft
and gentle towards your subjects; be their helper, so that
they shall be safe and sound. Know your duty, and understand
what it means to wear the crown. Be joyous in heart and read
these words often. Be humble, so that you will know God.]

5 James VI and I

The earliest poem attributed to James VI is entitled *The King's
verses when he was fyfteene year old* (i.e. written in 1581). It illus-
trates the troubled state of mind which the King experienced as
a result of his political initiation:

Since thought is free, think what thou will
O troubled heart, to ease thy pain!
Thought unrevealed can do no ill,
But words past out turn not again.
Be careful, aye, for to invent
The way to get thine own intent. . . .

> Since fool haste is not greatest speed,
>> I would thou shouldest learn to know
> How to make virtue of a need
>> Since that necessity hath no law.
>>> With patience then see thou attend
>>> And hope to vanquish at the end.

Most of James's poetry was written while he was a youth and a young man in Scotland, surrounded by a coterie of Court poets, of whom the most distinguished was Alexander Montgomerie, a kinsman of the royal House, who influenced the King's verse-making as well as enjoying his patronage. To Montgomerie James addressed a humorous *Admonition to the Master Poet to bewarr of Great Bragging Hereafter*:

> Give patient ear to sumthing I man say,
> Beloved Sanders, Maistre of our art.
> The mouse did help the lion on a day;
> So I protest ye take it in good part,
> My admonition coming from a hart
> That wishes well to you and all your craft,
> Who would be sorrie for to see you smart,
> Though other poets trowes ye be gone daft.

Perhaps it was under the influence of his 'Beloved Sanders' that James VI achieved a creditable mastery of the sonnet form, which in the late sixteenth century was as fashionable in Scotland as it was in England. One of James's best sonnets, addressed to his eldest son Prince Henry, is on the subject of kingship:

> God gives not Kings the style of Gods in vain
> For on his throne his sceptre do they sway,
> And as their subjects ought them to obey
> So kings should fear and serve their God again.
> If then ye would enjoy a happy reign
> Observe the statutes of your heavenly King,
> And from his Law make all your laws to spring,
> Since his lieutenant here ye should remain.
> Reward the just, be steadfast, true and plain;

Repress the proud, maintaining aye the right,
Walk always so as ever in his sight
Who guards the godly, plaguing the profane.
And so ye shall in princely virtues shine
Resembling right your mighty King Divine.

James was also capable of writing lyric verse, and a pleasant example is the song addressed to his unknown bride Anne of Denmark, which he wrote before he sailed across the North Sea to marry her in 1589:

What mortal man may live but hart*
As I do now, such is my case.
For now the whole is from the part
Divided, each in divers place.
　The seas are now the barr
　Which make us distance farr,
　That we may soon win narr†
　God grant us grace.

After his accession to the English throne in 1603, James wrote poetry less frequently. A late example of his verse is a poem on the death of Anne of Denmark in 1619:

Thee to invite the great God sent a star,
Whose nearest friends and kin good Princes are;
For though they run the race of men and die,
Death serves but to refine their majesty.
So did my Queen from hence her court remove,
And left the earth to be enthroned above.
Thus she is changed, not dead; no good Prince dies,
But like the daystar only sets to rise.

---

* but hart – without love.　　　† narr – near.

CHRONOLOGICAL LIST OF SCOTTISH SOVEREIGNS

The House of Dunkeld

DUNCAN I
born about 1001
reigned 1034–40
married a kinswoman of Siward, Earl of Northumbria,
name unknown

MACBETH (Maelbeatha)
born about 1005
reigned 1040–57
married Gruoch

LULACH ('the Simple')
born about 1032
reigned 1057–8

MALCOLM III ('*Ceann Mor*')
born about 1031
reigned 1058–93
married i) Ingeborg of Orkney
ii) St Margaret

DONALD BAN
born about 1033
first reign 1093–4

DUNCAN II
born about 1060
reigned May–November 1094
married Etheldreda of Dunbar

DONALD BAN
  second reign (with EDMUND) 1094–7
  died in, or after, 1099

EDGAR ('the Peaceable')
  born about 1074
  reigned 1097–1107
  unmarried

ALEXANDER I ('the Fierce')
  born about 1077
  reigned 1107–24
  married Sibylla, illegitimate daughter of Henry I of England

DAVID I
  born about 1080
  reigned 1124–53
  married Matilda of Huntingdon

MALCOLM IV ('the Maiden')
  born 1142
  reigned 1153–65
  unmarried

WILLIAM ('the Lion')
  born 1143
  reigned 1165–1214
  married Ermengarde de Beaumont

ALEXANDER II
  born 1198
  reigned 1214–49
  married i) Joan of England
         ii) Marie de Coucy

ALEXANDER III
  born 1241

reigned 1249–86
married i) Margaret of England
ii) Yolande de Dreux

MARGARET ('the Maid of Norway' or 'Damsel of Scotland')
born 1283
reigned 1286–90
unmarried

INTERREGNUM 1290–2

JOHN BALLIOL
born about 1250
reigned 1292–6
married Isabella de Warenne

INTERREGNUM 1296–1306

The House of Bruce

ROBERT I ('the Bruce')
born 1274
reigned 1306–29
married i) Isabella of Mar
ii) Elizabeth de Burgh

DAVID II
born 1324
reigned 1329–71
married i) Joan of the Tower
ii) Margaret Logie

The House of Stewart

ROBERT II
born 1316
reigned 1371–90

married i) Elizabeth Mure of Rowallan
ii) Euphemia of Ross

ROBERT III
born 1327
reigned 1390–1406
married Annabella Drummond

JAMES I
born 1394
reigned 1406–37
married Joan Beaufort

JAMES II
born 1430
reigned 1437–60
married Marie of Gueldres

JAMES III
born 1451
reigned 1460–88
married Margaret of Denmark

JAMES IV
born 1473
reigned 1488–1513
married Margaret Tudor

JAMES V
born 1512
reigned 1513–42
married i) Madeleine of France
ii) Marie de Guise

MARY, QUEEN OF SCOTS
born 1542
reigned 1542–67
married i) François II of France
ii) Henry Stuart, Lord Darnley

iii) James Hepburn, fourth Earl of Bothwell
executed 1587

JAMES vi
born 1566
reigned in Scotland 1567–1603

The House of Stuart

JAMES vi and i
reigned in Scotland and England 1603–25
married Anne of Denmark

CHARLES i
born 1600
reigned 1625–49
married Henrietta Maria of France

INTERREGNUM 1649–60

CHARLES ii
born 1630
crowned in Scotland 1651
reigned 1660–85
married Catherine of Braganza

JAMES vii and ii
born 1633
reigned 1685–8
married i) Anne Hyde
        ii) Mary of Modena
died 1701

WILLIAM 'iii' and MARY ii
William born 1650   Mary born 1662

Mary reigned 1689–94
William reigned 1689–1702

ANNE
  born 1665
  reigned 1702–14
  married George of Denmark

Exiled Stuarts

JAMES 'VIII and III'
  born 1688
  died 1766
  married Maria Clementina Sobieska

CHARLES EDWARD ('Charles III')
  born 1720
  died 1788
  married Louise of Stolberg

HENRY BENEDICT ('Henry IX')
  born 1725
  died 1807
  unmarried

COMPARATIVE DATE LIST OF ENGLISH SOVEREIGNS

Canute   1016–35
Harold I ('Harefoot')   1035–9
Hardicanute   1039–42
Edward ('the Confessor')   1042–66
Harold II ('Godwinsson')   1066
William I ('the Conqueror')   1066–87
William II ('Rufus')   1087–1100
Henry I   1100–35
Stephen   1135–54
Henry II   1154–89
Richard I ('Cœur de Lion')   1189–99
John   1199–1216
Henry III   1216–72
Edward I   1272–1307
Edward II   1307–27
Edward III   1327–77
Richard II   1377–99
Henry IV   1399–1413
Henry V   1413–22
Henry VI   1422–61
Edward IV   1461–83   (Henry VI restored October 1470 to April 1471)
Edward V   1483
Richard III   1483–5
Henry VII   1485–1509
Henry VIII   1509–47
Edward VI   1547–53
Mary I   1553–8
Elizabeth I   1558–1603

CHRONOLOGY OF PRINCIPAL EVENTS

AD

c. 500   Kingdom of Scottish Dalriada founded by Fergus More mac Erc.

563   St Columba founds his monastery on Iona.

685   Ecfrith of Northumbria defeated by Brude, King of the Picts, at battle of Nechtansmere.

843   Union of Picts and Scots under Kenneth MacAlpin, King of Scots.

943   Relics of St Columba brought to St Andrews.

1018   Lothian annexed by Malcolm II.

1034   Accession of Duncan I, founder of the House of Dunkeld; Strathclyde annexed to Scotland.

1040   Duncan I defeated and slain by Macbeth.

1057   Macbeth defeated and slain by Malcolm *Ceann Mor*.

1069   Marriage of Malcolm *Ceann Mor* and St Margaret.

1072   Malcolm *Ceann Mor* takes oath of homage to William I of England.

1093   Malcolm *Ceann Mor* ambushed and slain at Alnwick.

1094   Duncan II made King of Scots with English assistance, and in the same year overthrown and murdered.

1098   Western Isles ceded to Magnus Barelegs, King of Norway, by Edgar, King of Scots.

1124   Accession of David I, youngest son of Malcolm *Ceann Mor* and St Margaret.

1138   David I defeated at the 'Battle of the Standard'.

1139   Northumbria ceded to Earl Henry, son of David I, by Stephen, King of England.

1153   Death of David I.

1154   Malcolm IV forced to cede David I's gains to Henry II of England.

1174   William the Lion, King of Scots, captured by Henry II and forced to acknowledge him as overlord of Scotland.

1189   William the Lion recovers the independence of Scotland by the 'Quitclaim of Canterbury'.

1192   Pope Celestine III declares the Church in Scotland under the direct protection and jurisdiction of Rome.

1237   Tweed–Solway line agreed by Alexander II, King of Scots, and King John of England, as border of Scotland and England.

1249   Alexander II plans conquest of Western Isles, and dies suddenly.

1263   Alexander III, King of Scots, defeats Haakon, King of Norway at battle of Largs.

1266   Western Isles ceded to Scotland.

1286   Death of Alexander III.

1290   Death of Margaret, 'the Damsel of Scotland', the last of the House of Dunkeld.

1292   Edward I of England arbitrates in succession dispute and names John Balliol as King of Scots. Balliol pays homage to Edward I.

1295   Balliol repudiates his allegiance to Edward I.

1296   Balliol is forced to surrender his kingdom, and is imprisoned in England.

1297   Sir William Wallace defeats the English at battle of Stirling Bridge.

1298   Wallace defeated by Edward I at battle of Falkirk.

1305   Wallace captured by English and executed in London.

1306   Murder of 'the Red Comyn' by Robert Bruce; coronation of Bruce as Robert I.

1307   Robert I victorious at Loudoun Hill. Death of Edward I.

1309   Robert I receives declarations of loyalty from clergy and nobility of Scotland.

1314   Robert I defeats Edward II at battle of Bannockburn.

1320   The 'Declaration of Arbroath' addressed by Scottish nobility to Pope John xxii.

1328   Treaty of Northampton: England acknowledges sovereign status of Scotland.

1329   Death of Robert i.

1331   David ii crowned; the first Scottish King to be anointed.

1332   Battle of Dupplin Moor: supporters of David ii defeated by Edward Balliol.

1333   Supporters of David ii defeated by Edward iii at battle of Halidon Hill. David sent to France.

1341   David ii returns from France.

1346   David ii defeated and captured by English at battle of Neville's Cross.

1349–50 ⎱
1361–2 ⎰ The 'Black Death' in Scotland.

1371   Death of David ii, second and last king of the House of Bruce. Accession of Robert ii, founder of the House of Stewart.

1373   Act of Succession in favour of descendants of Robert ii by his first marriage.

1384   Robert ii's eldest son, John, Earl of Carrick, appointed his father's deputy.

1385   Scotland invaded by Richard ii of England.

1390   Death of Robert ii; John, Earl of Carrick, succeeds as Robert iii.

1399   Robert iii delegates his authority to his elder son David, Duke of Rothesay.

1401   Rothesay arrested.

1402   Rothesay dies mysteriously at Falkland; Scots defeated by English at Homildon.

1406   Robert iii's younger son James sent to France; captured on voyage by English. Death of Robert iii; accession of captive James i. Robert, Duke of Albany, Governor of Scotland.

1420   Death of Albany. His son Murdoch succeeds as Governor.

1424 Return of James I from captivity in England.

1425 Execution of Murdoch, Duke of Albany.

1426 Foundation of court of Justice later called 'the Session'.

1437 Murder of James I.

1440 The sixth Earl of Douglas and his brother murdered at the 'Black Dinner'.

1452 Murder of eighth Earl of Douglas by James II.

1455 Douglases defeated by James II at battle of Arkinholm.

1460 James II accidentally killed at siege of Roxburgh.

1463 Edward IV of England plots with ninth Earl of Douglas and the Lord of the Isles to partition Scotland.

1466 *Coup d'état* by Boyds; capture of James III.

1469 Marriage of James III to Margaret of Denmark; estates of her father Christian I in Orkney and Shetland pledged for her dowry.

1472 Orkney and Shetland annexed to Scotland. St Andrews becomes primatial see.

1482 Edward IV recognizes James III's brother Alexander, Duke of Albany, as 'Alexander IV' of Scotland. James III's favourites hanged at Lander Bridge.

1488 James III murdered after battle of Sauchieburn.

1494 Foundation of Aberdeen University.

1496 James IV invades England on behalf of Perkin Warbeck.

1503 Marriage of James IV and Margaret Tudor.

1507 Introduction of printing press to Scotland.

1511 Pope Julius II forms 'Holy League' against France; James IV faces consequences of alliance with France and England.

1513 War with England; James IV defeated and slain at battle of Flodden.

1514 Marriage of Margaret Tudor and sixth Earl of Angus.

1515–25 Governorship of John, Duke of Albany.
1525–8   James v the captive of his stepfather Angus.
1528   James v seizes power by *coup d'état*. Execution of Patrick Hamilton, first Protestant martyr in Scotland.
1535   Papal ratification of inauguration of 'College of Justice' in Scotland.
1537   Marriage of James v and Madeleine of France. Death of Queen Madeleine.
1538   Marriage of James v and Marie de Guise.
1540   James v circumnavigates the north of Scotland.
1542   James v dies after Scots defeated by English at battle of Solway Moss. Birth and accession of Mary, Queen of Scots.
1544–5   English invasions of Scotland: 'the Rough Wooing'.
1546   Murder of Cardinal Beaton.
1548   Mary, Queen of Scots, sent to France.
1558   Marriage of Mary, Queen of Scots, and Dauphin François (later François ii).
1560   Deaths of Marie de Guise and François ii. Reformation rebellion in Scotland.
1561   Return of Mary, Queen of Scots, to Scotland.
1565   Marriage of Mary, Queen of Scots, and Henry Stuart, Lord Darnley.
1566   Murder of Riccio. Birth of the future James vi.
1567   Murder of Darnley. Marriage of Mary, Queen of Scots, and Bothwell. Deposition of Mary. Coronation of James vi.
1568   Flight of Mary, Queen of Scots, to England; imprisonment of Mary by Elizabeth i.
1570   Death of Regent Moray.
1571   Death of Regent Lennox.
1572   Death of Regent Mar.
1579   Arrival in Scotland of Esmé Stuart.
1581   Execution of ex-Regent Morton; Esmé Stuart created Duke of Lennox.

1582	The 'Raid of Ruthren'; James VI imprisoned by Earl of Gowrie.
1583	James VI escapes from 'Ruthren Raiders' and asserts authority with assistance of Captain James Stewart, created Earl of Arran.
1585	Fall of Arran.
1586	Formal league between James VI and Elizabeth I.
1587	Execution of Mary, Queen of Scots.
1589	Marriage of James VI and Anne of Denmark.
1592	Murder of the 'Bonnie Earl of Moray'.
1595	Exile of Francis, Earl of Bothwell.
1600	The 'Gowrie Plot', possibly a conspiracy against James VI.
1603	Death of Elizabeth I and accession of James VI as James I of England.
1607	An abortive Act of Union passed by Scottish Parliament and rejected by English Parliament.
1612	Death of Prince Henry, elder son of James VI and I.
1615	Execution of Patrick Stewart, Earl of Orkney.
1617	James VI and I revisits Scotland.
1618	The 'Five Articles of Perth'.
1625	Death of James VI and I. Act of Revocation by Charles I.
1633	Charles I visits Scotland, to be crowned in Edinburgh.
1637	Imposition of Revised Prayer Book provokes riot in Edinburgh.
1638	The signing of the National Covenant.
1639–40	The Bishops' Wars.
1642	Outbreak of Civil War in England.
1643	'Solemn League and Covenant' signed between Scottish Covenanters and English Parliamentarians.
1644–5	Montrose attempts to win Scotland for Charles I.
1645	Montrose defeated at battle of Philiphaugh.
1646	Charles I surrenders to Scots army in England at Newark.

1647   The 'Engagement' between Charles I and moderate Covenanters.

1648   Defeat of Hamilton at battle of Preston.

1649   Execution of Charles I. Montrose invades Scotland on behalf of Charles II. Montrose defeated in Carbisdale and executed.

1651   Charles II crowned at Scone.

1651   Charles II defeated by Cromwell at battle of Worcester. Charles escapes to France.

1660   Restoration of Charles II.

1661   Scottish Parliament passes Act Recissory, annulling all legislation since 1633.

1666   Covenanters rebel; routed at Rullion Green.

1669–72 Lauderdale issues Declarations of Indulgence.

1679   Murder of Archbishop Sharp of St Andrews; Claverhouse defeated by Covenanters at Drumclog; Covenanters defeated by Monmouth at Bothwell Bridge.

1685   Death of Charles II.

1686   James VII and II grants freedom of worship to Catholics by royal prerogative.

1687   Freedom of worship extended to Quakers and later to Presbyterians.

1688   The 'Glorious Revolution' leads to the deposition of James VII and II.

1689   William 'III' and Mary II become joint sovereigns. Battle of Killiecrankie.

1690   'Revolution Settlement': 'Lords of the Articles' abolished; Presbyterianism official religion of Scotland.

1692   The Massacre of Glencoe.

1694   Death of Mary II.

1698–1700 Darien Expedition.

1701   English Parliament passes Act of Settlement in favour of Hanoverian Succession.

1702   Death of William 'III'.

1704   Scottish Parliament passes Act of Security – conditional repudiation of Hanoverian succession. English Parliament coerces Scotland by means of Alien Act and proposes Union.

1707 The Treaty of Union becomes law.

1714 Death of Queen Anne, the last reigning monarch of the House of Stuart.

Chronology of the Exiled Stuarts

1701 Death of James VII and II; Louis XIV of France recognizes his son as James 'VIII and III'.

1708 Abortive Jacobite rising.

1715 Jacobite rising, in favour of James 'VIII and III', led by John, Earl of Mar. Battle of Sheriffmuir.

1719 Abortive Jacobite rising defeated in Glenshiel. Marriage of James 'VIII and III' to Maria Clementina Sobieska.

1720 Birth of Prince Charles Edward Stuart.

1725 Birth of Prince Henry Benedict Stuart (later Cardinal York).

1735 Death of Maria Clementina Sobieska.

1745 Jacobite rising on behalf of James 'VIII and III' led by Prince Charles Edward.

1746 Prince Charles Edward defeated at battle of Culloden; extinction of Jacobite hopes.

1766 Death of James 'VIII and III'.

1772 Marriage of Prince Charles Edward to Louise of Stolberg.

1788 Death of Prince Charles Edward.

1807 Death of Cardinal York, last representative of legitimate male line of House of Stuart.

1 THE HOUSE OF ALPIN

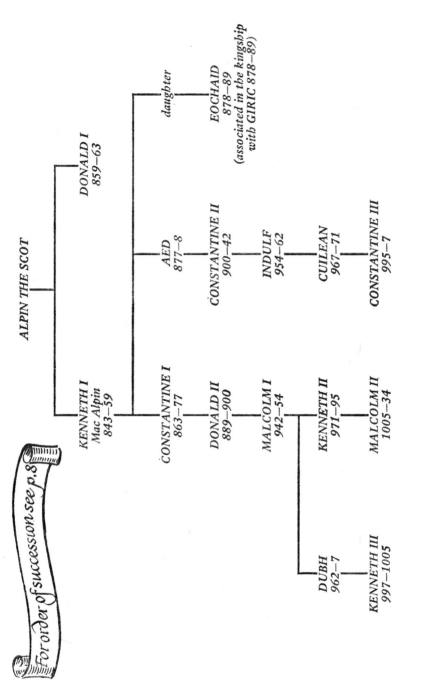

For order of succession see p.8

ALPIN THE SCOT

KENNETH I
Mac Alpin
843–59

DONALD I
859–63

daughter

EOCHAID
878–89
(associated in the kingship
with GIRIC 878–89)

CONSTANTINE I
863–77

AED
877–8

DONALD II
889–900

CONSTANTINE II
900–42

MALCOLM I
942–54

INDULF
954–62

KENNETH II
971–95

CUILEAN
967–71

MALCOLM II
1005–34

CONSTANTINE III
995–7

DUBH
962–7

KENNETH III
997–1005

2 THE HOUSE OF DUNKELD

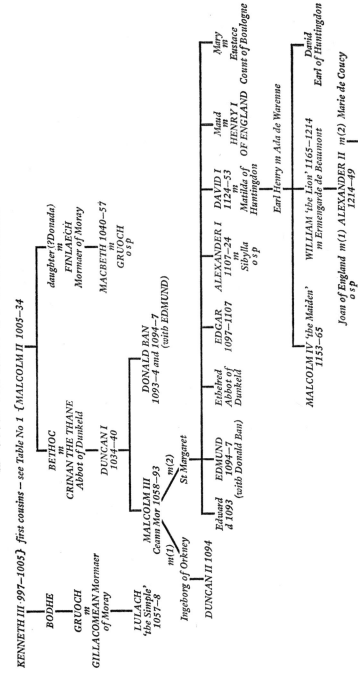

KENNETH III · 997–1005} first cousins – see Table No 1 {MALCOLM II 1005–34

BODHE

GRUOCH
m
GILLACOMGAIN Mormaer
of Moray

LULACH
'the Simple'
1057–8

daughter (?Donada)
m
FINLAECH
Mormaer of Moray

MACBETH 1040–57
m
GRUOCH
o s p

BETHOC
m
CRINAN THE THANE
Abbot of Dunkeld

DUNCAN I
1034–40

DONALD BAN
1093–4 and 1094–7
(with EDMUND)

MALCOLM III
Ceann Mor 1058–93

m(1)   m(2)
Ingeborg of Orkney   St Margaret

DUNCAN II 1094

Edward
d 1093

EDMUND
1094–7
(with Donald Ban)

Ethelred
Abbot of
Dunkeld

EDGAR
1097–1107

ALEXANDER I
1107–24
m
Sibylla
o s p

DAVID I
1124–53
m
Matilda of
Huntingdon

Maud
m
HENRY I
OF ENGLAND

Mary
m
Eustace Count of Boulogne

Earl Henry m Ada de Warenne

MALCOLM IV 'the Maiden'
1153–65

WILLIAM 'the Lion' 1165–1214
m Ermengarde de Beaumont

David
Earl of Huntingdon

Joan of England m(1) ALEXANDER II m(2) Marie de Coucy
o s p   1214–49

ALEXANDER III
1249–86
m(1) Margaret of England
m(2) Yolande de Dreux
(no surviving issue)

3 THE SCOTTISH SUCCESSION:

Showing the principal competitors, and the connection of the House of Dunkeld with its successors, Balliol, Bruce and Stewart.

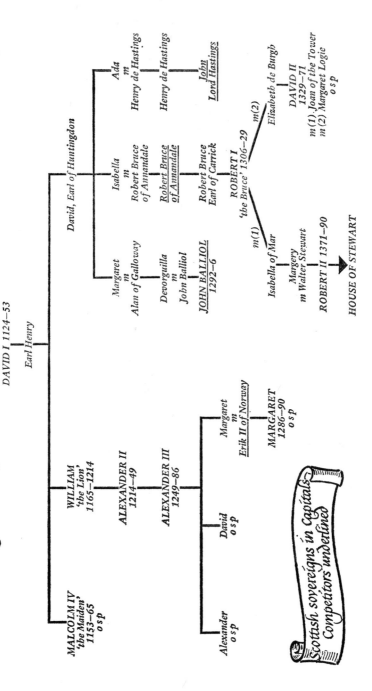

DAVID I 1124–53

Earl Henry

MALCOLM IV 'the Maiden' 1153–65 o s p

WILLIAM 'the Lion' 1165–1214

ALEXANDER II 1214–49

ALEXANDER III 1249–86

Alexander o s p

David o s p

Margaret m Erik II of Norway

MARGARET 1286–90 o s p

David, Earl of Huntingdon

Margaret m Alan of Galloway

Devorguilla m John Balliol

JOHN BALLIOL 1292–6

Isabella m Robert Bruce of Annandale

Robert Bruce of Annandale

Robert Bruce Earl of Carrick

ROBERT I 'the Bruce' 1306–29

Ada m Henry de Hastings

Henry de Hastings

John Lord Hastings

m(1) Isabella of Mar

Margery m Walter Stewart

ROBERT II 1371–90

HOUSE OF STEWART

m(2) Elizabeth de Burgh

DAVID II 1329–71 m (1) Joan of the Tower m (2) Margaret Logie o s p

Scottish sovereigns in Capitals
Competitors underlined

4 THE HOUSE OF STEWART

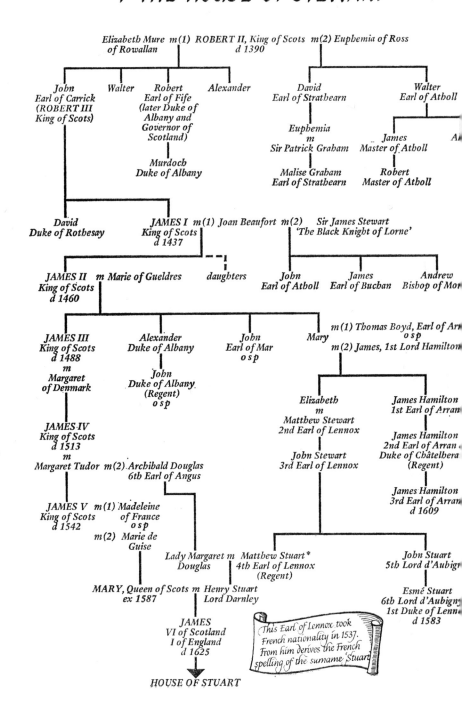

5 THE HOUSE OF STUART

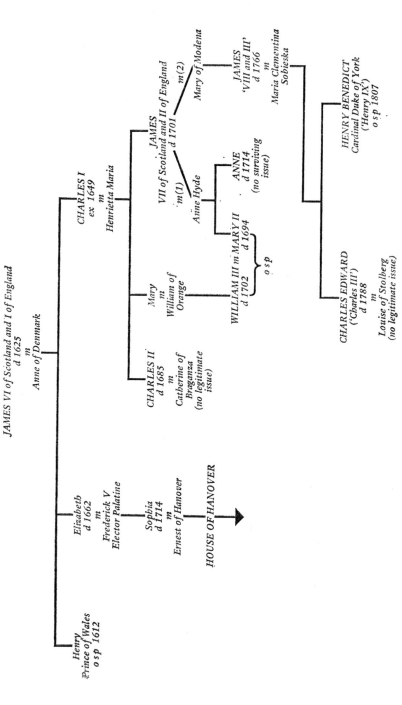

JAMES VI of Scotland and I of England
d 1625
m
Anne of Denmark

Henry
Prince of Wales
o s p 1612

Elizabeth
d 1662
m
Frederick V
Elector Palatine

Sophia
d 1714
m
Ernest of Hanover

HOUSE OF HANOVER

CHARLES I
ex 1649
m
Henrietta Maria

CHARLES II
d 1685
m
Catherine of
Braganza
(no legitimate
issue)

Mary
m
William of
Orange

JAMES
VII of Scotland and II of England
d 1701
m (1)
Anne Hyde

m (2)
Mary of Modena

WILLIAM III m MARY II
d 1702   d 1694
} o s p

ANNE
d 1714
(no surviving
issue)

JAMES
'VIII and III'
d 1766
m
Maria Clementina
Sobieska

CHARLES EDWARD
('Charles III')
d 1788
m
Louise of Stolberg
(no legitimate issue)

HENRY BENEDICT
Cardinal Duke of York
("Henry IX")
o s p 1807

Books Recommended for Further Reading

Since *Kings and Queens of Scotland* is intended as an introduction to the royal *dramatis personae* of Scotland's past, rather than as an introduction to the larger theme of Scottish history, this note on books recommended for further reading concentrates upon biographies wherever possible. Recent books, which it is hoped that the reader will find readily obtainable from the majority of libraries, are listed in preference to older works.

On the earlier Scottish sovereigns there is insufficient personal information for full-length biographies of individual figures to be possible. Some general books, however, can be recommended.

Who Are The Scots? edited by Gordon Menzies (BBC, 1971) covers the period from pre-history to the Wars of Independence, and contains the following sections by separate contributors: *The First Peoples* by Stuart Piggott; *Metal Workers* by Graham Ritchie; *The Roman Frontier* by Anne S. Robertson; *The Problem of the Picts* by Isabel Henderson; *The Scots of Dalriada* by John Bannerman; *Britons and Angles* by D.P. Kirby; *The Early Christian Church* by Charles Thomas; *The Norsemen* by David M. Wilson; *Anglo-French Influences* by G.W.S. Barrow; *The Making of Scotland* by A.A.M. Duncan.

Scotland the Nation by Rosaline Masson (Nelson, 1934) incorporates as much personal information as possible on the early Scottish kings, derived from chronicles and record sources. *The Story of Scotland* by Janet R. Glover (Faber and Faber, 1960) also has its emphasis on the influence of personalities.

Alexander III is the earliest Scottish King to be the subject of a biography, though *Alexander the Third, King of Scotland* by James Fergusson (Maclehose, 1937) has long been out of print.

* Books marked with an asterisk, published before World War II, may now be available only from major libraries, or through the library loan service.

171

Robert I has been the subject of several biographies. A recent and excellent one is *Robert Bruce and the Community of the Realm of Scotland* by G.W.S. Barrow (Eyre and Spottiswoode, 1965).

Scottish Kings by Gordon Donaldson (Batsford, 1967) is a survey of the Scottish monarchy from the House of Dunkeld to the Union of Crowns.

Most of the members of the House of Stewart have been the subject of full-length biographies, the exceptions being Robert II, Robert III, James II and James III. *The Stewart Kingdom of Scotland, 1371–1603* by Caroline Bingham (Weidenfeld and Nicolson, 1974) provides a short biography of each of the Stewart sovereigns.

Some biographies of the pre-Reformation Stewart Kings are **James I, King of Scots* by E.W.M. Balfour-Melville (Methuen, 1936); *King James IV of Scotland* by R.L. Mackie (Oliver and Boyd, 1958); *James V, King of Scots* by Caroline Bingham (Collins, 1971). A biography of Margaret Tudor, consort of James IV, appears in *The Sisters of Henry VIII* by Hester W. Chapman (Jonathan Cape, 1969). There is, unfortunately, no adequate biography of James V's second Queen, Marie de Guise, the mother of Mary, Queen of Scots.

There are innumerable biographies of Mary, Queen of Scots, but the major recent one is *Mary, Queen of Scots* by Antonia Fraser (Weidenfeld and Nicolson, 1969). *Mary, Queen of Scots* by Gordon Donaldson (English Universities Press, 1974) gives a very lucid explanation of the Scottish political background.

Various biographies of James VI and I have appeared during recent years: *The Making of a King: The Early Years of James VI and I* by Caroline Bingham (Collins, 1968) is a study of his childhood and youth up to 1583; *James I* by David Mathew (Eyre and Spottiswoode, 1967) gives an excellent account of his reign in Scotland and subtle evaluations of the leading figures of his reign in both Scotland and England; *King James VI and I* by D.H. Willson (Jonathan Cape, 1956) gives a somewhat unsympathetic portrait of the King.

Short studies of all the sovereigns of the House of Stuart are provided in *The Stuarts* by J.P. Kenyon (Collins, 1958). Brief and richly illustrated biographies of all the Stuarts have recently appeared in the *Kings and Queens of England* series published by Weidenfeld and Nicolson: *King James VI of Scotland I of England* by Antonia Fraser (1974); *Charles I* by D.R. Watson (1972); *Charles II* by Christopher Falkus (1972); *James II* by Peter Earle (1972); *William and Mary* by John Miller (1974); *Queen Anne* by Gila Curtis (1973).

Among more detailed studies of the Stuart sovereigns the best modern account of Charles I is still that given in *The King's Peace, 1637–1641* (Collins, 1955), *The King's War, 1641–1647* (Collins, 1958) and *The Trial of Charles I* (Collins, 1964), by C.V. Wedgwood. At the time of going to press, a new, major biography of Charles I by John Bowle was in preparation, to be published by Weidenfeld and Nicolson.

Some recent biographies of Charles II are *Charles II: The Man and the Statesman* by Maurice Ashley (Weidenfeld and Nicolson, 1971); *The Tragedy of Charles II* by Hester W. Chapman (Jonathan Cape, 1964). *James II* by F.C. Turner (Eyre and Spottiswoode, 1948) remains the best biography of the last Stuart King of the direct line.

William III by S.B. Baxter (Longman, 1966) and *Mary II, Queen of England* by Hester W. Chapman (Jonathan Cape, 1953) study the joint sovereigns separately; a joint biography is *William and Mary* by Henri and Barbara van der Zee (Macmillan, 1973). A good recent biography of the last Stuart monarch is *Queen Anne* by David Green (Collins, 1970).

Biographies exist of most of the Stuart consorts: *Anne of Denmark* by Ethel Carleton Williams (Longman, 1970); *Henrietta Maria* by Carola Oman (Hodder and Stoughton, 1936); *Mary of Modena* by Carola Oman (Hodder and Stoughton, 1962). The emotional lives of the Stuarts have been entertainingly and perceptively studied in *The Stuarts in Love* by Maurice Ashley (Hodder and Stoughton, 1963).

The exiled Stuarts have been the subject of innumerable books, and Prince Charles Edward in particular has been a popular biographical subject. Three recent good biographies are: *James* (i.e. James 'VIII and III') by Peggy Millar (Allen and

Unwin, 1971); *Bonnie Prince Charlie* by Moray Maclaren (Rupert Hart-Davis, 1972); *The Cardinal King* by Brian Fothergill (Faber and Faber, 1958).

Two recent general histories may be recommended, to provide an overall view of Scottish history: *A Concise History of Scotland* by Fitzroy Maclean (Thames and Hudson, 1970) is an outline history with many illustrations; *A History of Scotland* by Rosalind Mitchison (Methuen, 1970) is a vigorous and stimulating survey of Scotland from pre-history to the present.

Finally, *The Scottish Nation*, edited by Gordon Menzies (BBC, 1972), covers the period from the Wars of Independence to the Union of 1707. It contains separately contributed sections on the following subjects: *Wars of Independence* by G.W.S. Barrow; *Crown in Jeopardy* by Ranald Nicolson; *Taming the Magnates?* by Jennifer M. Brown; *National Spirit and Native Culture* by John MacQueen; *Flodden and its Aftermath* by Caroline Bingham; *John Knox and Mary, Queen of Scots* by Ian B. Cowan; *James VI and Vanishing Frontiers* by Gordon Donaldson; *Montrose and Argyll* by Edward J. Cowan; *Restoration and Revolution* by Rosalind Mitchison; *Union of the Parliaments* by T. C. Smout.

Index